The
Power
OF THE
Elevation
OF
Consciousness

BOOK 1: SOUL RESTRUCTURING

The Power

Power

OF THE

Elevation

OF

Consciousness

==

BOOK 1: SOUL RESTRUCTURING

Release disease, pain and suffering through awareness of the True Self

by

Johanna Bassols

Healers of the Light LLC 2018

ISBN-13: 978-1-7320832-0-2 (paperback)
ISBN-13: 978-1-7320832-1-9 (hardback)
ISBN: 978-1-7320832-2-6 (e-book)

Dedicated to all those great masters in my life

who led me to this moment.

Preface

The Power of the Elevation of Consciousness series is a compilation of theory and practical exercises in three books, that lead the reader to experience true awareness and to trigger changes in their perception of reality as a result of reaching a higher level of consciousness.

These changes restructure the entire soul imprint, the chemistry of the cells, and the whole structure of functions in the body. This allows us to experience awareness of the true self - a state of being in which we are free from identification with disease, pain, suffering and fear. We can then move from a perception of reality in which we live to satisfy sensorial needs triggered by brain impulses to one in which we are in control of all our elements and functions.

This book contains more than just written information. The exercises and practice make it an interactive experience and create a nexus of community with all of those who embark on the mission of bringing enlightenment and higher consciousness to our lives and to the collective as a result of our interconnectedness.

The book is complemented with a workbook to help the reader to keep track of their progress in the practice of the exercises shown here. It can be found at the end of the book and is also available for download on our website **https://healersofthelight.com/book-1/**.

This entire course is also available in our online school. Visit our website https://healersofthelight.com for more information.

Contents

Introduction

The purpose of this book is to help you return to the state of being in which you are free from disease, pain, suffering and fear by simply becoming aware of your true nature, the true self.

To activate this state of being, we will explore the science of the elevation of consciousness, leaving nothing aside, explaining the mechanics of the spirit, soul, brain and body, while also approaching it from a practical way to remove any filters and blockages to self-awareness. As you move along the pages of this book, you will become your own healer and your own guide in the process of the elevation of consciousness by awakening in yourself the awareness of being.

Have you ever felt that everything around you is changing fast, but you are still the same? Or like time is going faster, technology improves every second of the day? Ideas are there, but you have trouble accessing them on time?

You are right.

The world is changing faster than you can process it, but that is only a perception from a lower level of consciousness, observing a reality that belongs to a higher level of consciousness in which the entire planet and cosmos is already resonating, but that you have not accessed yet.

Once you step into the next level of consciousness, you are immediately in a new timeline of reality. You are no longer slow and outdated, but new, fresh, and able to access higher levels of the mind and heal yourself with your own consciousness of being as a perfect, eternal, and immortal self.

Even if your physical body dies, you still live because you are not the body.

This is not a work of magic; it is a work that requires recognizing yourself and embracing your presence in all its aspects, by living in awareness, triggering changes in the chemistry of the cells in the entire body and brain, by maintaining a conscious lifestyle, and continuing the expansion of consciousness to resonate at the unison of the universal evolution. All of this is described in detail in this series of three books, with practical exercises and meditations that help you reach awareness and change your perception of reality.

The first book of the Elevation of Consciousness series, *Soul Restructuring*, contains the theory and technique on how to recognize your own presence and your connectedness to everything else, experiencing oneness, through the state of awareness. Making emphasis on how to clear the soul from any blockages, emotions, or other filters that may affect that experience of recognizing the true self.

The second book, *Cellular Activation*, works around your habits of lifestyle, eating, thinking and behaving, reprogramming them to trigger important cellular changes that will allow you to interact with higher frequencies, programs, people in your life, events, and others.

In the third book, *Elevation of Consciousness*, we explore in detail the process of the elevation of consciousness to continue expanding your reality, unlocking the true potential of all your organs, energy centers, mind, and soul.

Throughout the books, you will reinforce the wisdom acquired with the application of practical exercises that will lead you to the activation of your energy centers and of important stimuli to achieve elevation of consciousness.

Elevated consciousness changes your perspective on life, allowing you to release the false belief of all that is not the true self: disease, pain, suffering and fear.

Let's see how this works. On to chapter 1!

The True Self

Section 1: *Finding the True Self*

When we are born, we believe that everything we see is true. Later on, we learn to believe that everything that our parents believe is true. Then we go to school, and we learn to believe that everything we learn at school is true.

And we go on like for this for our entire lives, collecting beliefs that sympathize with this hybrid perception of reality that we have formed.

Every belief that you acquire, every identifier that you add to the perception of yourself is one more layer of separation from the true self.

Each belief and each identifier make that which is true seem false, not because truth can ever be false, but because it can be perceived as such.

Separation from the truth is the only thing that can make you believe that disease is true, that conflict is true, that pain is true, but these are all false beliefs. These are beliefs that are not the true self, and that which is not the true self is false and cannot exist.

But how did we get to this point of living a perception of falsehood? How did a subjective perception get so far that it became a rule in the human world?

We inherited this perception of reality and adopted it as true.

We inherited this reality, and we choose to continue believing it as true, suffering the consequences of denying the true self.

We walked in a reality in which the self is mortal, is temporary, is sick, is angry, is evil, and we created a set of rules to protect ourselves from these beliefs. We made others believe them too, until finally, the entire world believed the same thing.

But how did this start? Why would someone create a perception of false self? With what purpose?

The reasons could be many; people living in fear can submit to institutions of power like religion, political regimes, and medicine. Historically, humans have always struggled with domination. We either dominate others or are dominated by them, and the best way to impose dominion is by implanting fear, by spreading false beliefs about the self.

If everyone knew the power that self-awareness and being fully conscious holds, they would not need to be ruled, healed or guided by anyone else other than themselves, and this is far too risky for those who are in a position of power.

This has happened since the beginning of history; it is not exclusive to the present figures of power, although this model is used to this day. The spread of new diseases followed by vaccination campaigns; social discordance and magical politicians who coincidentally can solve those very same issues; economic depression, followed by the rise of new billionaires; and so on. They are only implanted beliefs. If you fall for them, it could set you even further apart from the truth.

The same thing happens between the perception and realization of ourselves. These are the two polarities of the same process of awareness. A perception of ourselves involves beliefs, identifiers, and filters, and the realization of ourselves is a state of being, the truth beneath all those ideas.

In these man-made ideas about ourselves, we could believe that disease, pain, suffering and fear are true. We believe this because we were taught that it is true, and never question it. Even if we have never experienced it, we still believe it and make it exist in our reality.

Some others have experienced these ideas and believe them to be true, but it was only because they believed in them, that they existed in their reality. But if the same person becomes aware of the true self, this person will heal himself.

The only instance in which we can be ill, imperfect, or mortal is when we believe that we are anything other than the true self. Once we recognize ourselves through awareness, we can return to the state of being in which we are fully present, embodying the true self, and revert the false perception of reality that our beliefs could have caused.

We can summarize this search for awareness of the true self in four paths:

1. **Through initiation or DNA activation:** DNA activation is a consequence of awareness. When awareness is sustained for long periods of time, or constantly triggered, DNA activation occurs; this allows the embodiment of the true self. We become it.

   When the holographic DNA is connected, we are again aware of our spiritual nature. This path requires mastering awareness as a stimulus to reach awareness as an active state of being. In other words, finding the way of manifesting yourself.

2. **The path of detachment:** When we stop satisfying the needs of the ego, we become stronger than the brain impulses that demand the actions to satisfy sensorial needs. That which we believe is what gives sense to our life. We detach from accumulating possessions, from all things that are temporary and are not the true self.

   This doesn't mean that we must live in austerity; it only means that our perception changes to one of detachment from those temporary things, relationships, or circumstances.

   By going further away from that which is not true and is temporary, we get closer to the true self.

   Detachment also means leaving behind the results of our actions. That is not the true self. We are not what we do; we are what we are.

3. **The path of self-control:** We realize that we are more than our body and mind once we learn how to control them. There is a way to communicate with the mind and body to become the true self through that interaction. Through controlled breathing, movements, and meditation, we can connect to the awareness of the true self.

4. **The path of immersion into the life of the self**: This means that we become devoted to living a life in which we practice all these paths to awareness, embodying the true self, detaching from the temporary, and becoming the masters of our own mind and body. This is a spiritual path that requires sacrifices, only when seen from the point of view of someone who has not yet encountered the true self. Once the true self arises, there is no sacrifice; there is only the joy of being.

In this series, we will explore these four paths for an integral approach to awareness. You may be more inclined to one of them than the others, and you can always develop that interest further once you have been introduced to these forms of expression of the self.

Section 2: *Differentiating True from False Self*

One of the hardest things that we must endure during our life in the physical form is living a perception of reality that doesn't recognize the existence of the true self. Some of the pain and suffering that we experience in this form is originated from ignorance of the true self, and the rest comes from our decision to deny its existence.

* * *

When we choose to believe that the temporary aspects of reality that we experience on earth are true and define us, we are also giving that temporary aspect to ourselves. And that makes us vulnerable to anything of that nature.

The true self is not limited by time or space.

It is beyond any words that can define it and beyond any quality of the physical reality.

We can't define the true self through the senses because the senses are of the body.

We can't define it through the mind because the mind is of the soul.

We can only experience it through awareness of the spirit.

* * *

The true self can't be defined in any terms that can be defined themselves.

The true self can't be identified with any identifiers.

The true self can't be heard with human ears.

It can't be seen with human eyes.

It can't be smelled, touched, or felt.

* * *

The true self can't be found in one place or in a time frame.

The true self can be experienced in the spirit all at once, in its holographic form through awareness.

It can be seen in the arts but not in its physical expression, only in what originated the arts.

It can be seen in the human, but not in its body, only in what created the human.

It can be seen in the words, but not in their literal meaning, only in their semantics.

* * *

The true self can be experienced in the oxygen that we breathe, but not in its physical attributes, only in the life it gives us.

It can be experienced in the light, but not in its physical attributes, only in the guidance we receive from it,

It can be found in the dark, but not in its physical attributes, only in the unmanifested reality that it holds.

It can be found in intelligence, but not in knowledge,

in the water but not in wetness,

in the fire but not in the heat,

in the air but not in its coolness or freshness,

in the earth but not in its texture or density.

It is in everything that we touch, yet it can't be felt with our hands.

It is in everything that we hear, yet it can't be perceived with the ears.

It is in everything that we smell, yet it can't be sensed with the nose.

It can be spoken, but it's not a word.

It can be sung, but it's not a song.

It is in life, but not in death.

* * *

The true self is our most pure essence; it never changes, despite the forms that we embody searching for it.

The true self is formless.

When we choose to define the true self, then we are saying, we too are that.

When we accept disease, pain, or suffering as true, we are saying, we too are that.

When we accept confusion or doubt as true, we are saying, we too are that.

When we accept chaos or conflict as true, we are saying, we too are that.

When we deny the true self, we deny ourselves, and that makes us false and consequently we can no longer exist.

We sentence ourselves to death every time that we deny the true self.

The true self is eternal.

The true self is immortal.

The true self is unmanifested reality.

The true self is Universal Intelligence.

I am that I am.

I am that I am.

I am that I am.

Section 3: *The Unmanifested Reality*

There are instances in which we become so disconnected from our spiritual aspects that all we can perceive is the tangible reality. We lose all awareness of the true self; we accept the false beliefs as true and become those beliefs.

* * *

We accept that something that is temporary and circumstantial is true, and that which is true exists in our perception of reality.

We accept that we are mortal, and that which is true exists in our perception of reality.

We accept that we are in pain, and that which is true exists in our perception of reality.

We accept that we are suffering, and that which is true exists in our perception of reality.

What we allow in our reality becomes our world while that perception of reality exists.

* * *

Your world is only available to you; it's the sum of all your beliefs and experiences recorded based on those beliefs.

Your world was given to you by your ancestors, and you shaped it with even more beliefs.

Your world only accepts beliefs that resonate with the collection of beliefs that you already have acquired or adopted as yours from your ancestors.

Your world can never be seen from the outside; it is an inner perception.

Your world can never be explained to others because they will only understand it from the perspective of their own worlds.

Your world can change when your beliefs change.

* * *

Separation from the spirit form is necessary because it is only in the absence of spirit that we can find spirit.

Spirit doesn't need to find itself.

Spirit is aware of itself.

Spirit knows what is true and what isn't, and that is why it remains alive, immortal, and eternal after the physical body dies.

Spirit is the true self.

Spirit knows the manifested reality; it has experienced it in other forms: as a frequency, as a physical body, and later, as a soul.

Spirit searches for the unmanifested because there it can find true eternity and limitless expansion.

Spirit is looking for that which can never change, just like when we search for spirit while in the physical form.

The search of Spirit for the unmanifested is a mirror image of our search for spirit; it is the same process in different expressions of itself.

Spirit is multidimensional.

Only spirit can allow us to experience the unmanifested reality.

* * *

The unmanifested is that space of **the Universal Mind** where everything comes from, the space that creates the manifested reality.

The unmanifested is intelligence; it is creation; it is life force.

The unmanifested is the darkness before the light, the creation before the idea, the place where nothing can ever exist, yet everything that exists comes from it.

Only in the unmanifested reality we can experience the full awareness of ourselves as creators, as Godhead, divinity.

To reach the unmanifested we must be aware of the true self, spirit, for only spirit can access the unmanifested reality.

* * *

Before we say a word, that inspiration is in the unmanifested reality.

Before we write a book, that inspiration is in the unmanifested reality.

Before we dance, that inspiration is in the unmanifested reality.

Before we express ourselves in any way, that inspiration is in the unmanifested reality.

* * *

Our essence is limitless, infinite, and eternal, yet we choose to identify with time, space and death, only because these are beliefs that we inherited, beliefs of the observable reality that is not us.

Form is only an aspect of us - in a self-imposed illusion of reality to help us find ourselves, and only then, return to the unmanifested.

Why would we want to identify with disease, conflict, chaos, and expiration when we can identify with expansion, eternity, and abundance?

It is only a matter of changing our beliefs.

But the true self can't be found in the mind either. By changing our beliefs alone, we won't find the true self.

We need to change our beliefs only to allow us to experience awareness of the true self.

The true self cannot be perceived when there are clutter, blockages, filters, and ideas that prevent us from experiencing it.

We need to go through a process of soul restructuring before we can experience awareness of the true self.

CHAPTER 2:
The Soul

Section 1: *Soul Restructuring*

Restructuring means changing the structure of the soul, its elements, and the way its layers are arranged, releasing anything that could be attached to it in the form of a belief, emotion, or memory that separates us from the truth.

The new soul structure is something that happens naturally once we can release the old, stagnated elements that respond to functions of the lower levels of consciousness. This allows new elements to take their place and arrange themselves according to the new dharma, or new cosmic order, dictated by the forces of evolution.

This new organization of the layers of the soul works more effectively than the old structure. It's equipped with the right combination of structure and programming to allow us to perform, interact, process, and absorb the higher frequencies that are present already in the cosmos because of the evolutionary shift. The simpler it gets, the better for its performance.

This is the focus of our study and practice in this book, restructuring the soul to experience awareness of the true self, and through this experience heal ourselves.

Soul restructuring is also the first step toward the elevation of consciousness, a stimulus and a process in which we embody the true self and live in the physical world from this perception of reality. Returning to the original idea of the true self can reestablish our elements to their original state of health and balance.

The original idea of the true self, the breath of life, can be perceived through awareness and presence. It can be practiced and maintained for longer periods of time to become a stimulus for the activation of the holographic DNA.

DNA activation unlocks our true potential as physical and spiritual beings.

For the effects of this entire course, when I talk about DNA activation, I'm referring to strands of phantom DNA that are not active in our system. Scientists have identified them as "junk" because they can't physically observe their behavior.

When you activate your DNA, you transition your entire operating system from a brain stimulus-based system to a DNA stimulus one, which is powered by the heart center. In the lower levels of consciousness, all of our processes happen through brain stimulus. The brain constantly sends impulses to satisfy sensorial perceptions. We become the servants of the brain stimuli unless we can deactivate these impulses and migrate to a higher consciousness system.

Once you are able to deactivate the sources of unnecessary brain stimuli such as foods that contain any sugar or that are addictive in nature, and release addictive thoughts and emotions with the process of soul restructuring, you can begin to bring awareness to DNA impulses that serve as better activators of stimuli. Consequently, you can reach enhanced abilities and performance while connecting to a higher consciousness.

After the DNA impulses are active and the brain can fulfill its ordinary functions more effectively, we are no longer subject to the chemical processes of the brain that provoke movement, cravings, desires, and sensorial needs; instead we focus on programs of a higher level of consciousness that involve the well-being of others and are not only centered on "I."

With this process our consciousness expands and becomes aware of what is around us, changing the priorities from a self-centered perspective to a much larger one.

The DNA stimulus sends signals to the brain and the other organs to perform functions according to higher consciousness. Even physiological needs become of a higher nature. We eat to nourish the body not to satisfy the senses; we act in love, not from sexual impulse; we sleep with a purpose to heal the body not from laziness.

When we deactivate the unnecessary brain impulses to migrate to a DNA impulse-based system, we still utilize the brain, but not in the way that we are used to now: not by reaction of stimulus of the brain itself that responds to sensorial needs created by chemistry of the food and addictive thoughts, behavior and memories, but by command of the heart center. The goal is to attain full awareness of the true self, to elevate the consciousness, and then from that place, develop the full potential of the brain. But while being blinded by the everyday needs of sensorial perception, the brain is unable to develop such abilities.

This transition requires not only awareness of the spirit, but also of all the activities that we perform in the physical level. It commands changes in our eating habits, social interaction, exposure to spaces and people, and others.

By adopting these changes and changing our beliefs, we can reset our old cellular structure to interact with much higher frequencies, making us more resistant, and preventing the malfunction of our systems.

These cellular changes are deeply discussed in the second volume of *The Power of the Elevation of Consciousness: Cellular Activation. There,* we explore how to change the chemistry of the brain and body through dietary changes, breathing, and movement. We learn how to stimulate the main cell production centers to procure good health and to improve the capacity of those cells as containers of higher frequencies, programs, and information.

Cellular activation is another necessary process to attain the elevation of consciousness. Only in an environment in which we have restructured our soul, cells and beliefs, can we trigger the stimulus of the elevation of consciousness that takes us to the embodiment of the true self, as expressed in our new perception of reality.

The elevation of consciousness is both a stimulus and a process. When all the conditions are given for our perception of reality to change, we experience awareness, DNA activation, and the stimulus of the elevation of consciousness all in one, in a holographic form. This is what starts the elevation of consciousness as a process.

The process consists of a series of levels and rounds that expands our perception of reality at the same time that our DNA expands its volume in a perfect equation equivalent to 1.1618 angstroms per time.

All the details about the process of elevation of consciousness are described in the third volume of the series.

To effectively work with the soul, we need to understand its structure.

The soul is composed of various layers of elements, some with electromagnetic properties that protect and energize the physical body, some that work as receptors and transmitters of frequencies, and others that perform the inherent functions of each layer. The boundaries between layers are given by the functions of its elements, although they are not clearly delimited, as there are elements that constantly travel between layers.

When seen from an elemental view, there is no separation between body and soul, or between us and anything else; we are constantly exchanging elements with everything that we encounter, including the environment and external influences from other beings.

The physical body and the soul are all part of the same organism, but at the moment of physical death, the body and soul separate, and the elements that form part of the physical body dissolve to go back to their source in the earth elements, while the elements of the soul may remain grouped temporarily to then separate and go to many different places. Some of them stay on the earth level, some others merge with elements of nature, and still others start looking for the path to return to the immediate source that created them: stars, planets, ether, the mind, etc. Only the spirit remains and continues the path of the elevation of consciousness in the levels of the spirit.

The spirit, being the only true essence, is the only element able to continue ascending in its levels of consciousness until it can become fully aware of itself as the unmanifested reality.

For this study, we will work with five layers that are the closest to the physical body.

1. **The astral body:** This is the closest layer to the physical body. It has autonomy of functions, although it is connected to the physical body for the duration of the life of the body. It is responsible for protecting it and gives the last revision and approval or rejection to the frequencies with which we come in contact, before they can reach the physical body.

   This prevents us from developing disease or other conditions. It also absorbs energies that can heal the physical body and applies them to it as needed.

   When the physical body is sick, the astral body becomes thinner and lowers its frequency. If we use resources like Kirlian photography to see the expansion of our aura when we are sick and compare it to a time in which we were in good health, we can see that the energy field looks thinner, weak or has dark stains as if there were holes in it.

   The astral body takes the toll of a disease before the physical body can even sense any effects, and in this same way, the outer layers of the soul process those toxic frequencies first, before they can reach the astral body. Some of these frequencies can come from the outer layers themselves, in the form of negative emotions or thoughts.

   The stronger the soul structure is, the lesser the chance of falling ill or developing any conditions that affect our overall health that we will have.

2- **The mental body:** This layer is immediately above the astral body and contains elements that store information.

The mind, as it's mostly understood, is this layer of the soul.

The Universal Mind, on the other hand, is the source of all ideas; it doesn't exist inside our brain, although we can connect to it through the brain. We could also connect to the Universal Mind through the heart or other organs that serve as antennas for this purpose. We don't have any control over the Mind, only over the mental body.

When we have repetitive thoughts, we are dealing with brain stimulus that connects us to information stored in the mental body over and over.

The mental body as well as the astral body are autonomous and can interact with other elements on their own without needing to use the physical body. The mental body is a full representation of the physical body in a mental aspect, and the astral body is a representation of the physical body in its etheric aspect. The inverse is also true, the physical body is a representation of the mental or astral bodies in their physical aspect.

3- **The psychosomatic body:** This layer is located between the mental and the emotional bodies of the soul. It serves as a union between both and filters the information that comes from the physical body or from external sources to distribute it to either layer.

    This layer can determine what emotions are released and which ones are transformed into other impulses. It is an important layer for our study of the soul and the release of both emotions and thoughts..

4- **The emotional body:** This layer stores emotions in three elemental forms: core emotions, substitutes, and drafts. We will study these in depth when we get to the release of emotions section.

    We can say that emotions are not originated in the soul, but come from the secretion of organs that cause specific reactions in the body, and are recorded in this layer of the soul according to that effect: fear, sadness, anxiety, etc.

The emotional body can replicate those emotions, triggered by brain impulses, at any time, without having to create a new emotion or without any apparent reason.

Memories can also trigger emotions stored in the emotional body; there is no need to have a new experience to produce the same emotional effect, although its intensity may be lower than that of a core or original emotion. We already lived the core emotion when we experienced an event the first time. What we experience with a memory is a substitute emotion of less intensity.

5- **The forming body:** This layer is formed by various elements of the soul and of the electromagnetic field that is right above it. This is a layer of protection that filters any frequency that meets us, before it can be processed and sent to the other layers of the soul, or to the brain or body.

It is called forming body because it is in constant formation, absorbing elements of the frequencies that we meet. It also has electromagnetic elements that protect the soul from the direct effect of these frequencies, only allowing in what is necessary.

This structure in five layers is optimal for the best performance of the soul instead of other systems with more layers and more divisions of functions and elements that could potentially cause delays and miscommunication between the layers. This realignment of the layers happens naturally when the elements of the New Order start to integrate with the soul; they purge the old ones and rearrange themselves in this position.

Besides these five layers we also find the electromagnetic field that surrounds the entire soul, protecting it from external influences. It is formed as a reaction caused by the friction of the soul and the atmosphere, and it is in direct contact with the forming body.

This is one of the most evident reasons why soul restructuring and the entire process of the elevation of consciousness is needed. We have already started to observe the effects of these external influences from evolutionary changes in the forms of disorders, diseases, health conditions of all kinds, and confusion. Our beliefs, stagnated energies, emotions, and accumulated identifiers create blockages that prevent these evolutionary changes from taking effect. Once we release them, we can fully interact with the new frequencies, absorbing their benefits instead of rejecting them.

The goal of these frequencies is to activate awareness and self-recognition, as we evolve toward enhancing our spiritual aspects and awakening; but when they can't get past the layers of beliefs, emotions, and other blockages that stand in the way, they directly affect the body and soul functions instead.

These evolutionary frequencies are more powerful than the protective shield of the soul. The forming body can only effectively process what its current structure allows it to. Everything else is absorbed and processed by the other layers in any way they can, and what can't be processed goes directly to the physical body, causing adverse effects.

Soul restructuring is the proactive way of healing the soul to allow it to receive these frequencies, absorbing its benefits and new elements to replace the old, obsolete ones.

During the process of the elevation of consciousness, we observe additional changes in the soul structure due to the expansion the DNA that affects all of our aspects, including the soul.

We can describe this process as an expansion in volume of the DNA molecule. DNA expands in observance of the Golden Ratio, a 1.618 increase of its overall magnitude with each level of consciousness. It has been determined that the DNA molecule measures in size 34 angstroms long by 21 angstroms wide, yet there's not much said about the fact that it expands in a very subtle, but determinant, way when consciousness also expands.

These same numbers can be found in the spiral forms that we see in nature and have been very well been pointed out by the mathematician

Leonardo Fibonacci. When we divide these two numbers, we obtain the golden ratio 1.618 which is the measure of expansion of DNA and hence, of consciousness

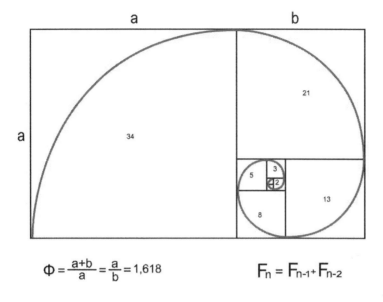

$$\Phi = \frac{a+b}{a} = \frac{a}{b} = 1{,}618 \qquad\qquad F_n = F_{n-1} + F_{n-2}$$

Figure 1: FIBONACCI NUMBERS. The Golden Spiral

This is important for our understanding of the mechanics of consciousness, but as anything else in science, it happens regardless of our understanding or our even knowing about the matter. What we do need to know is how to interact with this process to allow it to occur in us, by removing any filters and blockages that may stop, slow or prevent the elevation of consciousness.

Consciousness is in the spirit, which remains intact after the physical body dissolves, and even after the soul separates from the spirit, and can be directly influenced by the holographic DNA.

The spirit is protected by both the layers of the soul and the physical body. To get to it efficiently, we need to work our way in — starting from the exterior layers and moving inwards toward the body. That's the reason why I have arranged the volumes of *The Power of Elevation of Consciousness*, in a way that allows you to work on the soul first, then the body, and finally, on the embodiment of the spirit.

To achieve higher consciousness, we need to be aware of our entire being, not only of the spiritual aspects of it. We must realize and honor the physical body, as well. We are all that in one, and all that which we perceive as external, too; there are no "others".

This is the process of the elevation of consciousness, in which we are aware at first of our physical aspects, then our perspective, and reality grows to realize our spirituality, and from there to realize our connection to everything there is, as us, the true self. This is the path to eternity. When you realize that you are in everything and in nothing at the same time, and that for the unmanifested, there is no death.

Section 2: *Decluttering the Soul*

Our soul, body, and spirit are multidimensional expressions of the true self. We can change that expression according to what we believe to be true.

If we believe that anything other than the true self is true, then that becomes our reality and it exists for as long as our temporary belief lasts.

The only way of experiencing the true self is through awareness, but awareness cannot manifest itself in an environment that contains false ideas and blockages. It can only surface when all those conditions are removed and not replaced with any other belief, but simply removed to allow awareness to be experienced.

The true self then becomes our reality. Something that can't be explained with words, but that we know with blind faith because we experienced it in a level of awareness that explained any questions that we may have had about our existence.

To get us closer to experiencing the true self, we must restructure the soul. That means resetting it to a point of origin before we acquired any beliefs or identifiers that changed our original state of being.

Restructuring is a process that we will learn step by step, starting with identifying and releasing emotions, then rearranging each of the layers of the soul.

Emotions are the main group of elements that are stored in the soul and that can dramatically affect the way we perceive reality and how we manifest it.

From the level of human experience, we understand them for the reaction that they cause in our sensorial perception, whether it is fear, love, anxiety, depression, joy, etc. But when seen as elements in their raw form, emotions can represent more complex organisms.

In general, emotions are created by the secretion of organs that trigger a certain chemical reaction and are perceived by the senses in various forms. These original emotions created from the body are called *core emotions*. Once a core emotion is created, other elements with similar characteristics and effects in our sensorial perception are created by the soul, as well, to be able to replicate the effect of the emotion without an original cause, called *substitutes* and *drafts*.

The process of storing emotions observes the following structure:

1. **Core emotion:** This is the original emotion, created by the secretion of an organ (this includes glands) in the physical body, which then migrates to the soul in the form of an etheric element. A core emotion is an entity on its own, with autonomy and independence from the organ that created it, a living organism. The elements that form core emotions can leave the soul altogether after the event that triggered them is no longer in effect, but the soul has means to replicate them and reactivate these duplicate emotions when prompted by a stimulus. These are called substitutes and draft elements.

Core emotions are activated by a combination of factors:
   · Elements in the brain that send signals to parts of the body to secrete substances that create the emotion to satisfy a sensorial need.

- Elements in the cortex of the brain that activate the core emotion at will: It's in the cortex that the human will is housed.

- Elements in the pancreas and the gallbladder activate a group of emotions related to the lower part of the body.

- Elements in the heart and lungs activate emotions related to the middle section of the body, like the sensation of being in love that is felt in the heart: While the sensation of fear is felt on the lower part of the body, people can urinate when they are afraid. It also depends on the kind of fear that is activated.

- Elements in the eyes of a person can send an emotion to the eyes of another person and be received by the elements in the brain of the receptor, triggering the process of secretion of the corresponding organ. This is also present in the eyes of animals; when we look at a dog in the eyes, it can trigger the fraternal love emotion in us.

- There are groups of emotions linked to every organ and even to the blood. There are also emotions that are activated by the coenzymes in the saliva, which has important activators that travel throughout the organs that participate in digestion, triggering the secretion of substances that create emotions.

- Hormones also activate emotions in both men and women, in direct connection with the reproductive organs and the brain.

2. **Substitute emotions:** These are elements that resemble core emotions, and that can remain in the soul indefinitely after the core emotion vanishes. It's a duplicate that triggers the same response in the human body and brain but, with less intensity. It can be triggered by various stimuli, including brain stimuli and external influences.

    These are etheric elements that don't leave the soul because they are created directly in the soul, but they can be deactivated.

3. **Draft emotions:** These are elements that can activate a substitute emotion that is dormant. They are triggered by brain stimuli and, like the substitutes, they don't leave the soul. They are an intrinsic part of its structure, but they can be reset and deactivated.

These are the most significant activators of emotions. From an elemental level, we can say that emotions are not produced by external elements, but by internal processes. They can be triggered or stimulated by an external impulse, but in their creation, only the elements of our own body participate.

This helps us to understand emotions and to how to control them. Even if we have no control over the external circumstances that may have triggered the initial stimulation of the organs, we now know that unless our body produces the secretion of substances, there won't be any reaction.

This is significant because we do have control over our organs, glands, cells, and all the elements in our body. The fact that we are not used to commanding or ruling the actions of them doesn't take away our capacity to do so. We have witnessed in the history of eastern religion and spiritual practices, the level of control that these adepts could gain over their own body; this is not exclusive to a religion or group. This is possible to all who develop the practice of self-awareness and an understanding of the elements.

Emotions also have the characteristic of being etheric; they are not tangible or dense in any form, and because of that, they are subject to the rules of etheric elements.

Etheric is a quality of an element that refers to its density. These elements are mostly made of ether and remain in the etheric space during their entire existence.

When an organ starts the process of the secretion of substances that forms the emotions, it sends a stimulus to the soul in the form of etheric elements. These are processed and crystallized in the soul, which is also etheric, creating the substitutes and draft emotions. The emotional body is constantly activated by the secretion of organs and by brain stimuli.

To efficiently release all the elements of the emotions from either the body or the soul, we need to be aware of the connection between the organ that produces the initial secretion of fluids and how that translates into an emotion. This way, we can interrupt the process in various ways, reprogramming the organ, and teaching the organ that you have direct control over it.

Exercise 1: Identifying the source of emotions

In this exercise, we will learn to communicate with our organs to stimulate a response or suppress the process of the creation of a core emotion. To start, we need to have a clear view of which organs produce what kinds of emotions. There is no defined boundary between emotions and what kind of stimulus activates each one of them, but there are some general rules that we can use to identify them in groups.

Instead of trying to memorize a list of organs that trigger each emotion, use your perception of the emotion and identify where in the body it is perceived.

Where is the activity, pain, or movement when the emotion is active?

You can practice, if you wish, by triggering at will one or two emotions by activating a memory or thought that produces emotions.

Identify the origin of this emotion.

In what part of your body do you perceive the emotion?

Identify the section first —upper, middle, or lower body— and then try to determine a more specific place in the body.

Try to determine now where the emotion is going next. Do you feel the fluid going up or down? Or is it in the center of the organ, causing a sharp pain?

Take notes and develop this further. If possible, you should have a notebook or diary with you to make note of every emotion and its production center and path. Do this for a period of a month. This will help you identify the most typical emotions that you activate during the day.

Once you can neutralize that group, your clarity in front of new situations or in life in general will be completely different.

The organs on the superior part of the body, like the brain, throat, tonsils, and tongue, are in direct contact with the emotions like confusion, not belonging, and depression. You can feel the stimulus that causes the emotion of depression coming from these parts of the body, or perhaps in your case, it comes from a different part of the body, like the heart, because emotions are not clearly defined.

When we are in a rush and start feeling stressed and nervous, the first thing that happens is that you can't talk correctly —your tongue doesn't respond to your brain commands, there is confusion and dizziness. Then this reaction starts triggering other organs. If the emotion is not controlled in its initial stage, it could affect the entire body.

By using this technique of identification, we can immediately act by tapping on the specific area where the emotion is being felt to neutralize or calm it, to avoid the formation of a new core emotion, the activation of substitutes, drafts, or the spread to other parts of the body.

The organs in the middle section of the body, like the heart, lungs, spinal cord and thoracic cage, are directly related to emotions of love, compassion, or sadness, for example.

Emotions similar to these can be felt in other parts of the body, also triggered by other organs. Remember that in the elemental world, emotions are not defined by names. They don't need to fit a description given by us; they are a conglomerate of fluid coming from different organs or parts of the body that create etheric elements that can be perceived in different ways.

It is pointless to try to identify emotions by defined names and link them permanently to the organs that produce them once. Instead try to identify the sections of the body where the emotion is felt and be aware of how this makes you feel without necessarily giving it a name. This is all you need to know for the first part of this exercise.

I have included the thoracic cage in this group because although it is not an organ, it segregates substances from the membrane surrounding the cavity that also participate in the process of creating emotions.

The organs in the lower part of the body, such as the stomach, liver, lower internal organs, intestines, and reproductive organs are perhaps the most active in the production of emotions.

These organs are directly related to emotions of the sexual kind, fear, and others less defined. Sometimes we need to use several identifiers to describe the way we feel. Most likely, those kinds of emotions come from the lower part of the body.

Sometimes the organs, and even the soul, choose to create default systems or shortcuts to eliminate the daily need to run a full process from the start to create or trigger an emotion. These default systems are what form our behavior and temperament.

With this understanding of the origin of core emotions, we can help them dissolve. We can do that by establishing direct contact and interaction with the organ, by either tapping into it directly or visualizing that we are breathing through the organ in a fluid way, inhaling and exhaling consciously through the organ, observing the air go in and out of it.

This interrupts the process of the formation of the core emotion, lowering its effects and intensity.

* * *

The best way to neutralize an element is with another one of similar nature. They tend to understand each other, and the entire process is much more effective than introducing a foreign element. For example, anxiety could have more than one origin. There is no defined producing organ. That's why we can find some medicines that reduce its effects by triggering the production of stomach fluids, while some others act directly on the brain. This interrupts the organ and inhibits it from producing the secretion that causes the emotion.

This is the reason why some medicines work better than others, even though they are targeting the same thing. They trigger the production of fluids from different organs. It is a sort of gamble to know if they will target the right source.

You could also consciously activate positive emotions secretions in your organs as a daily practice and strengthen the organ with certain movements and localized breathing. This way of activating the organs is studied in detail in the second book of *The Power of The Elevation of Consciousness: Cellular Activation.*

To ensure that you are triggering the right neutralizing emotion, you need to understand the concept of polarity very well. This will help you work with anything at an elemental level.

Everything that exists, every element in the universe, observes the Law of Polarity. For example, the polarities of height are tall and short; the ones of temperature are hot and cold; the polarities of emotions are love and hate; or courage and fear, etc.

A good practice to soothe an emotion is to release its polar opposite. This creates an environment in the body that neutralizes or soothes its counterpart emotion when it starts to form. We don't need to wait to experience a negative emotion to want to stop it. This practice can reprogram the organs that produce negative emotions, learning that these are no longer needed. However, our goal after changing the chemistry of the body should be to find a mid-point or balance that we can sustain.

Extreme emotions are not sustainable; we would be fooled to think that we can live in extreme joy every second of the day. That would simply drain us out. Polar opposite emotions are needed to help us find balance. Balance is sustainable, and if from that place you experience extreme joy, you can always go back to the point of balance instead of experiencing a tremendous low after the joyful episode ends.

But to return to balance, you need to first; become familiar with the experience of balance, and that is directly related to the experience of awareness. Both of these coexist and are experienced at the same time.

With this practice of soul restructuring, you can clear the patterns that take you on extreme emotion roller coasters to find your point of balance.

The process of activating the production of positive emotions that we will learn in this volume of the series is through stimuli. It could be a brain stimulus, induced by visualization or by conscious command to the organ to act in certain way. It can also be manipulated with external substances that trigger the emotion that we want, like in the case of holistic herbs, or by tapping the organ in a special way that I will show you now.

Tapping is an ancient technique that has been used in holistic medicine for centuries to release stagnated energies and emotions. We can use it to either stop the secretion of fluids that produce negative emotions, or to activate those that produce positive ones.

Again, I emphasize that there is no need, nor is it effective, to target emotions by their specific kind; we will have much better results if we focus only on the experience without trying to give it a specific name and simply relate it to the section of the body where the stimulus comes from.

With this practice of identifying the origin of the stimulus, you will realize that emotions of a certain kind are always linked to that same section of the body. And if you lose interest in labeling it, you will be able to feel the emotion in its real proportion, without trying to make it be fear, or anxiety or panic when this is something of its own kind. You can call them emotions from the top, middle or lower body if you prefer.

This classification coincides with that of the energy centers that also have an immediate effect on the organs closer to them. As I mentioned previously, the new cosmic order brought in changes in all of our systems, that include not only the structure of the soul but the way in which we interact with energy, as well. Instead of working with a seven chakra system, we will be working with three energy centers located in the crown, heart, and navel.

Exercise 2: Tapping

When we tap over one of the energy centers, we trigger an energy flow of electrons and protons that stimulate the organs in that immediate section in a positive way. This releases any blockages of fluid or stagnated energies and helps us release any trapped emotions that could be forming in that center before being sent to the emotional body.

Tapping is simple, and consists of intermittent, firm, but gentle, taps and pauses, with one or two fingers directly over the organ, or energy center. You can practice this for periods of two to five minutes at a time and then move to another organ to promote healthy energy flow. Making sure to not miss the top of the head, the heart, and the navel, which are where the main energy centers are located.

This same practice can be applied to minimize the action of an organ when a negative emotion is in the process of formation. This speeds up the flow of energy and reduces the secretion of fluid of the organ or stops it altogether. The effect will depend on various factors, such as the power of the impulse, the time in which you start applying direct tapping, and how clear the energy centers are from other elements that block the energy flow.

This is why practicing this technique on a regular basis is recommended. It promotes healthy energy flow and prevents stagnated elements from staying stationary, either in the organs or in the energy centers.

Keep track of your progress in a daily journal; notice if emotions reduce their intensity after continuous tapping; note if they disappear. You can also use this technique when you feel pain in any of the organs. and observe how the pain immediately dissipates. Of course, this is ideal for mild pain; in the case of a life-threatening injury or situation, you should contact your doctor for immediate assistance.

Emotions can also be triggered by external impulses, and not only by the secretion of fluids of our own organs. This happens especially when we are exposed to certain levels of frequency that alter the normal environment of our energy field, or of the elements of the soul.

For example, when we are exposed to radiation or UV lights of any kind for an extended period, or in an abrupt way, our soul, which is our external layer of protection, together with the electromagnetic field, weakens, and as a consequence, we could observe direct effects in the physical body.

External impulses can trigger the organs directly to produce a core emotion, or they can activate existing elements in the soul, such as substitute or draft emotions.

On a daily basis, we interact with hundreds of frequencies, some more powerful than others, that can change our soul or even our cellular structure. For this reason, the more we practice reinforcing the layers of the soul and the electromagnetic field, the stronger we will be in front of energetic attacks.

In the case of the soul, the interchangeability of elements is much more evident because of its etheric nature, but the physical body also goes through this exchange every second of the day. We are not the same person at any given time. We are a conglomerate of elements, constantly merging, dissolving, and integrating into others. The only thing that keeps us together, or at least gives us the perception of density and separation, is our consciousness.

Even if you have not experienced awareness of the true self yet, your elements of the body and soul know it well and remain together in resemblance of it. This is the only identification that we never lose; all other things are temporary and can change in any moment.

In this process of soul restructuring, we aim to detach from the identification with that which is temporary. This doesn't mean that you literally have to break up with your parents and quit your job to find yourself; it means that although you are aware of those identifiers and honor them for the great service they provide you in your life on earth, you recognize that you are not them.

Your perspective is what changes, not the actual relationship with the identifiers. You can and you should find ways to coexist with all creatures at all levels of consciousness; that is part of your own journey. You have chosen the group of beings in your life to learn something from them. You need to find what that is and honor that process.

Some people do need to make changes in their relationships and in their work to find balance and get to the realization of who they are. Many people contact me daily for counseling on how to make this transition without hurting anyone involved, or without giving up on something that they fought so hard to build.

Lilian M. is a dear friend of mine from college who went through the loss of both of her parents in a tragic accident when we were in our last year before graduation. This was very painful for her, and she was unable to leave her house or even her bed for over a month. She was in deep reflection about the meaning of life and the time we have to find it.

She understood at that point that life was not to be taken for granted and she made the decision to leave everything behind—her studies, her relationship at the time. She gave up on most of the things she owned and disconnected from everything.

A few years later, I found her online as the coordinator of a non-profit organization that protects endangered species in Asia. I reached out to her, and I could hear in her voice a passion for life that very few people have. She was a totally new person. She had given up everything and started volunteering in various causes, all related to animal welfare. She gave up all identification with what she thought she was and gave herself to the service of the animals. She found so much love in that action that she never needed to look back.

"Giving up my false self allowed me to find my true self," she said. I couldn't be happier for her realization. She added that the level of consciousness (she called it level of spirit) in which she is now is the most powerful magnet to abundance and meaningful relationships. She has met wonderful people that supported her all along without expecting anything in return, which happens to be the same frequency that she is projecting when she gives her entire life to animal conservation without expecting anything from them.

The energy that she gives is mirrored and comes back to her in the ways that she needs to be helped.

I've also known many others who have made rushed decisions in times of peak emotions and have regretted them. The key is in neutrality—being able to make a decision or to take an action not influenced by emotions, but by pure awareness.

The answer is different for everyone, as everyone is in different processes and stages of that transition, but one thing is certain: No matter what changes go on in your life, the spirit never changes. The closer you could get to the awareness of the spirit the clearer you will see the path, and for that you need to be in control of your emotions.

Others choose to embark on pilgrimages, on journeys of many years with almost nothing, in search of this true self. Some spend years in silence, or meditating, or going through difficult situations in life that make them reflect one way or another.

There is no right or wrong way to get to the true self. If you are reading this book it is because you have chosen to find the true self, and this is one of the ways in which it is being presented to you. If you are in this situation, in which you feel the urge to make changes, before changing anything outside of you, work on your internal conflicts, blockages and stagnated emotions first. Restructure the soul, experience awareness and once you have already recognized your true essence, you will have all the necessary tools to go in the right direction.

If you are going to make permanent decisions that could change your entire life, you want to make sure you make them from a place of balance and higher consciousness. One should never make decisions when feeling anxious, nervous, excited, or happy. One should be balanced and neutral to experience awareness, and from there, act as ourselves.

Section 3: *The Evolutionary Process*

Because of the evolutionary shift, there are new frequencies in our space that trigger emotions and all sorts of reactions in the entire body, but that do not necessarily observe the process or stimulus of the organs.

This creates a problem for us, because we have more control over the function of our organs than we do over external stimuli. This happens every time the universe goes through an evolutionary shift or when we are exposed to radiation or UV rays from the damage in the ozone layer, or to other stellar influences. Over time, we became more resistant to this exposure and developed ways to interact with it more effectively. Although a lot of studies and protective measures were given to the physical aspect of these external influences, such as the many effects in the skin and tissues, not much was said about the influence of such exposure to the soul, and how it affects our behavior.

The best way to understand these influences is to study the relationship between the time of extreme exposure to these frequencies and the historical events occurring in those regions of the world most affected by them. You would be surprised to see the correlations of these.

UV rays are just a small example compared to what we are going through now. Since the beginning of the 21st century, we have been exposed to the frequencies of the evolutionary shift that affect the entire universe. These changes cause many different reactions in all forms of life. We can observe the rise of mental disorders, social discordances, polemic politics and media, revolutions in health and food and in the way that we recognize ourselves, coming more into contact with our spiritual aspects of the self.

We can't deny this influence brings a variety of emotions and stimuli, many of which are completely new for us, making us vulnerable, as we don't know how to process, or stop such stimuli. This is an expansion of the entire cosmos, and as such, it must revolutionize everything, including the structure of the human soul, our bodies, and the way that we interact with energies.

This influence can't be stopped; it is implacable. It is the power of the expansion of the universe. Life in itself is expanding to elevate its consciousness, and to elevate the consciousness of every element that is within it.

There is nothing we can do to prevent this, nor should we, because this influence is here to help us improve as a race, making us more endurable, stronger, and more connected to the true self, to the spiritual aspects of our being.

This is necessary for our existence on this planet and in this solar system, and the only thing you can do about it is to find out how to prepare yourself to integrate with it in a more harmonious way—receiving it, rather than rejecting it, and making good use of the benefits of evolution.

But how can we change from the inside out to allow interaction with the forces of the entire cosmos?

The best way is by doing the same thing that the cosmos is doing, emulating it, as above so below, and as within, so without.

By elevating our consciousness, we emulate the process of expansion of the universe. Consciousness is contained within our DNA and when it expands, the DNA expands too.

A full study of consciousness and its behavior is presented in the third book of The Power of The Elevation of Consciousness: Elevation of Consciousness. This is a process that involves soul restructuring, cellular activation, and the elevation of consciousness itself as a self-creating process.

For now, we will focus on the first part of this process, restructuring the soul to remove all blockages that prevent us from fully experiencing self-awareness to integrate with the "all" in a natural and harmonic way

Section 4: *Removing Blockages to Experience the True Self*

To fully experience the true self, we need to reach the state of awareness. Any blockages in the soul or body will act as filters to this experience and will not let us come to a full encounter with the true self.

It is important to clear every blockage from the roots to not have to deal with any other versions of the blockage later. This doesn't mean that you won't have to deal with other blockages later. In fact, you should be proactive and keep the soul and body clear at all times, but the higher your consciousness is, the easier it will be to maintain the balance by living fully present. The more you experience the truth, the less vulnerable you become to false beliefs.

Once you can release all blockages and experience awareness, you can begin the process of the elevation of consciousness. This requires that awareness is held or constantly stimulated until it activates the holographic DNA; after this, by keeping these two activators constantly stimulated, you can also activate the stimulus of the elevation of consciousness.

With the elevation of consciousness, you can experience reality as the true self, embodying it. With each level of elevation, you lose beliefs and blockages. Instead of adding anything, it takes away layers and layers of all false beliefs. We don't need to accumulate more to embody the true self. On the contrary, we need to let go of it all to make room for it to be fully manifested.

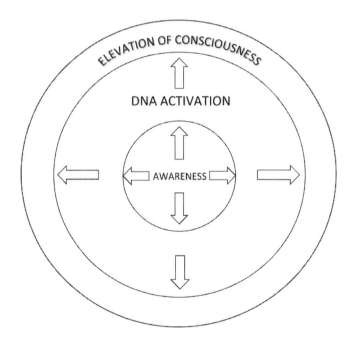

Figure 2: THE PROCESS OF ELEVATION OF CONSCIOUSNESS

The fact that there are blockages in the soul is irrefutable. We all have them. They can be stored at any given time, with any activity or thought, even during sleep.

How can we keep up with something so etheric that seems to have a life of its own?

We only need to create enough room to experience awareness and maintain it for long enough to convert it to a stimulus that activates the DNA. Once we can pass this initial process, the rest is on its way. Once you see the truth, you can't unsee it, but if you have never experienced it, it is easy to remain ignorant.

Once you experience the truth, everything else that is not the true self will simply start fading, as there is no room for identification with that which is false. It is like when your parents told you the story of Santa Claus —you believed in this, but once you learned the truth, you couldn't keep believing in Santa.

Our entire reality is based on stories that we were told, either from our parents, society, figures of power, or ancestors as old as the first humans on earth. We believe them to be true, until we experience the true self. Then suddenly, we can't continue believing what we were told, and instead believe what we have just experienced. The paradox of this is that when we are awakened to the truth, we often seem as if we have lost our minds; we are the ones out of reality by realizing the truth; which is only possible if what we believe as true is rather false.

If during this practice of the elevation of consciousness, you feel like your perception of reality has changed, and you may not fit in anymore with what you were doing or even with what you thought you were before experiencing awareness, you are on the right path. That means that your perception of reality is starting to shift. It is different than what your ancestors or immediate circle accepts as true, and you are opening to a more expansive, limitless view of yourself and of the meaning of life.

Fear is normal during this process, but you can overcome it by surrendering to that feeling, embracing it, expanding it as much as you can. It is just a new feeling that becomes familiar relatively fast. Instead of evading fear, consciously embrace it. You will see how it starts changing; it can't be sustained in awareness.

The elevation of consciousness is something that may take some time, but it is attainable. There is no set road or time frame. It is all open to your own ways of finding it and how much you really want to accomplish it.

The exercises in this book are a guide that you can use and follow at your own pace to experience an encounter with yourself.

For best results, you should not add to or remove anything from this process, as these are the most basic practices to reach awareness using this system that has worked for me and many others that come to me for counsel on a regular basis.

Do not practice other methods while you are practicing this, so as not to cause any sort of interference. Trust the process; trust yourself, and the result is just a consequence. Focus only on the process, not on the result or expect anything. Expectations are beliefs that cover up the real experience of awareness. The moment that you are completely free from every belief and keep the mind quiet is when you can really be aware.

Exercise 3: Identifying the true selfт

There are many ways of removing blockages, most of them focus on the actual blockage, but we have now learned that we can attain healing by focusing and bringing awareness to the state of being in which we are free from beliefs and identification with that which is not the true self. Instead of focusing on each blockage, we will focus on the true self, magnifying its presence and making that awareness so engraved in us, that everything else which is not true will begin to fade.

To start, take a pen and paper, and write on it the name that you were given at birth. Write your name and last name.

This is the first identification that we have when we are born. We know from the first days of our existence that we are that name. When you get asked on the street what your name is and who you are, the answer is the same—a first name and a last name. Now add to the list a few more identifiers that you have collected during your life until now.

What else do you identify with?

A country?

A family?

A profession?

A race or religion?

A gender?

A quality that you may have?

Write as many identifiers as you can, and this will help you realize how much you have to release. List the positive qualities and negative qualities in two separate columns, as we will use them in different ways.

Once you have completed the list, look at it for a few seconds.

Has there been a time when you were not one of these identifiers?

Before you became a doctor, professor, firefighter, were you still the same person?

Before you became a student, were you still the same person?

Before you began to identify with a particularly negative quality, were you the same person?

Probably, you will want to respond yes, but something tells you, *no, I'm definitely not the same person, after I became a doctor, or a teacher, etc.* And in some way, this is true. We are different every second of the day. We accumulate identifiers all the time. Our soul and body change and we transform with every single element that enters or leaves us, but there is something that never changes, that remains untouchable through time, regardless of the exposure that we may have to any external identifiers, and that is the true self, the spirit.

In a way, we are different every second of our lives, but in another, we are always the same, even if we can't perceive the true self because it is buried by identifiers, the true self continues to be true.

If we peel off these layers of identification with temporary elements, circumstances of the physical plane, and ideas, we can start seeing the light of the true self. The first signs of it are the positive qualities; the true self contains the sum of all positive qualities that a human can have, all that falls under the concept of humanity.

Now let's practice a visualization exercise:

Please find a comfortable sitting position, relax the body, and focus on your breathing for a minute or two.

Imagine that you are standing in the middle of a crowded plaza. You are completely naked. You have no possessions, no family or friends. You are surrounded by people who are looking at you with judgment and expressing their dislike for your immorality and lack of consideration for others by showing yourself so openly.

They are standing around you, and even if they think this is immoral, they stay to hear what you have to say. They are curious to know why you are exposing yourself in this manner, and they demand an explanation.

You remain there, standing without saying a word. They are starting to get anxious, and start asking all kinds of questions: *Who are you? What do you want? Why are you doing this?* They threaten to call the police.

After a few minutes, the police come and also demand an explanation: *Why are you standing here in your most basic form? Where are your clothes? The things that you own? Where is your family? What is your name?*

Then you decide to start talking, you say: *This that you see here is what no one wants to see, the one that we all are. We all have skin, bones, organs, a head, a heart, a stomach. We all are human, we all have a body like mine, a brain, a soul, a spirit and qualities that make us be human.*

In fact, we all share the same space on earth. We are in the same place at the same time, doing different things, living different illusions to then return to source, having learned more about who we are, yet we choose to believe that we are all those things that we accumulate in our lives on earth, and we waste our precious lifetime identifying with that which is temporary. And the story repeats again over and over until we finally realize we were not any of those things.

Then you ask the police officer: *How would you feel if you were not a police officer? Would you still be you?* Then you ask the street sales person:

What about you? If you were not selling things on the street, would you still be you?

They all respond: *Yes, but of course, what kind of crazy question is this? We would still be us.* Then you ask them to describe themselves without using any of the identifiers that they have acquired during their life on earth, and they simply can't answer.

Without that there is nothing left, they say. *We are what we do, what we have become with time, the legacy of our families and parents.*

And you respond: *Absolutely not! I am standing here today choosing to release all identification with those elements that came to me after I already was a true being, and I have never felt more alive than today.*

Those people in the plaza are your identifiers. They are surrounding you, trying to tell you, that you are them, something other than the true self, that there is nothing beyond what you have acquired here, but you know that this is not true because during all this time that you were standing there as a vulnerable, pure and completely free being, you were still you.

Each one of the identifiers on the list, is not you. The identifiers are simply circumstantial. They can be helpful or not during your life on earth, but it is imperative that you recognize their temporary nature. There is no need to try to idealize them as if they were true.

Now that you are standing in front of these judging elements and you see yourself bare, naked and free, what else do you see, besides the physical body?

You can put a name tag to each one of the people in the plaza with the identifiers on your list; you can also add to the list habits or negative qualities. If you can name it, it goes on the list.

What is left?

There is a physical body, our instrument in our journey on the earth that we ought to respect, nourish, and care for until our last day.

There is also a brain that connects the mind with the functions of the body and soul.

You have a heart, which allows the blood to flow everywhere. You have lungs that allow you to breathe, a tongue that allows you to eat and communicate, a mouth that also participates in that process, a face that helps you recognize your physical body; the hair on your head or no hair is also part of the identification of the physical body, as well as other attributes such as color of the skin, height, age, gender. All these are physical identifiers to help us differentiate from one another as part of the illusion of separation that we observe in the physical reality.

The physical body and all its qualities should also go on your list now, as they are not the true self either.

What else is there?

You have a soul.

What do you know about it?

Have you ever tried to see yourself as a soul and not a body?

We already know what the body is and does, and we know that we are very similar to all other humans as far as function and shape. Is there a chance that our soul has the same structure too?

The soul also has the same structure in everyone else. It has a set of layers that act as a shield for the physical body and carries the electromagnetic charge that gives life to all its elements.

The soul, just like the physical body and its organs, has a system that stores the identifiers that we collect during our life on earth.

For a better understanding of these systems, it is important to know some basic information about the structure of the soul. The layers of the soul are composed of elements of different kinds, with various functions. These elements are grouped, forming layers, and each layer is in direct correlation with the one above and below. They work as a sort of filter, cushion, decoder, and receptor of energy.

The frequencies or energies that enter the soul dissolve into millions of elements that then merge with our existing ones. They can also be rejected and pushed away, or they can stay in the periphery of our individual elements or of the entire field, forming an additional layer that filters anything else that comes in contact with us.

The subtle differences that we observe between us are only a product of these identifiers. We have some that come with us from even before incarnation that are needed for the development of our life purpose. The ones that we acquire here may also help the same goal. However, the problem is not the system, or how identifiers work, the problem is our identification with them.

If we didn't have those differences, we would be still functional. We can realize the usefulness of these identifiers, as they are useful but not necessary. We could accomplish the same thing from any angle without the circumstantial identifications.

All the identifiers of the soul should also go on your list, as the soul is not the true self.

What is left, then, after releasing the identification with everything that is on your list?

Just your name?

Let's get rid of that identification, too.

What if you decide to change your name today, would that make you feel different about yourself? Would that change who you are in any way?

Would you feel lost?

Perhaps from this level of perception of being used to your identifiers, you perceive it that way, but once you release them, you won't feel a need for identification with them any longer.

This point of zero identification is our goal. A point in which we recognize our identifiers, we are grateful for them, but we chose to not make them a defining aspect of us, rather simply a tool or circumstance.

When we lose the identification with these temporary elements, most of our problems disappear, as well as our blockages. We are saying, *this is not real,* and what is not real can no longer exist.

Practice this exercise of separating yourself from all identifiers every time you feel it's necessary, whenever you can perceive any sort of identification with all that is temporary. Put them on that list and spend a few moments with what is left, leaving only the positive qualities as those are part of the original idea of the true self, of the concept of humanity, that encompasses all qualities of being human, but only be aware of them.

Do not develop an identity either, and see how you feel. If any judgment comes up, write it down on the list, as it is only one more identifier.

Not all positive identifiers are positive qualities. For example, you may consider your socio-economic condition to be positive, but it's not a quality, it's an identifier. A quality could be something like honesty, patience, balance, serenity, truthfulness, etc.

Do this until nothing that you can put into words is left.

Spend five minutes every day with this realization. How does it feel?

Don't try to explain it with words, simply be aware of that feeling.

See how your relationship with everything else starts to change. Things may not have the same importance as before when you realize their temporary nature. The same will happen in your relationship with people; you will be able to notice when they are acting from one of these filters and when they are being unique and true.

You can choose to observe them from their core and not from their circumstances. If you find yourself formulating any kind of judgment, that is a form of identification that you are creating for them. It only blocks your perception of who they really are.

Try the same exercise with someone you love. Write down a list of all the identifiers that you perceived of them and let them go, knowing that those elements are merely circumstantial and do not define them either. This is only your perception of them, your identifiers and beliefs, not necessarily theirs. Now try to look at that person or imagine the person as if they were standing in front of you.

Can you still see them as before? Did your perception change? What emotions are you managing? Write down any judgment that comes to mind, and let it go knowing that this is not them.

Continue observing the person or image until you are left with something that you can't put into words.

This is their true essence. Does it feel like your own? How is it different? Perhaps there are a few more identifiers that you missed.

Try to spend some time with that notion of the person in their essential form, free from any identifiers.

Practice this. Imagine each one of your closest friends and relatives, even if they are already departed. Honor them for what they are. This will help you let go of all judgment, understanding that they could be going through a phase of identification with a circumstance, but that this is not really who they are. Once you experience the true self in them, you will be able to deal with each situation without forming judgments or beliefs about them.

This a way of removing the blockages that prevent you from seeing who they really are, if you can put the idea of them into words, those are identifiers and must be released.

Section 5: *Rearranging the Layers of the Soul*

The process of rearranging the layers of the soul for its best performance happens naturally, once you allow the release of old, obsolete elements and let new elements integrate into the soul structure.

It is important to practice the awareness of the true self on a regular basis. You can set up an alert in your calendar to remind you every day to meditate on this experience to get to this state of mind. With practice, the state of mind will transform into a state of being, and you will experience the activation of your holographic DNA.

Even if it is for five minutes at the beginning of your day, this will help you remain in balance, and all of the temporary things and circumstances will seem less and less important. When you master this technique, existing problems will dissipate completely, as nothing is a problem any longer—it is all temporary.

The same goes for emotions. Learning to identify where the stimulus that creates the emotions originates and tapping into that organ will help you reprogram the organ and lower the intensity and effect of such emotions until they are no longer a threat.

In this section, we will work on each layer of the soul, restructuring it and releasing blockages and obsolete elements to allow new, more efficient ones to evolve. For this we will use a technique that involves visualization and reinforcement with a physical action to activate the electrical impulses of emotions, memories, or thoughts to then release them through the process of grounding (or earthing).

In this first exercise, we will elevate the frequency of the electromagnetic field by releasing its old elements and allowing the new ones to integrate. We can ground the elements in a few different ways: once we activate the electrical charge of the emotion, memory, or thought, we can visualize how the electricity of that element moves in a circular motion, and instead of completing a full circle, it is grounded on the floor. We will use a representation of that process to make it more convenient and comfortable for our practice, using a bowl with dirt or soil instead.

If you prefer using the floor, you must be barefoot on the ground floor, ideally outdoors. The electricity of the process that we are activating in the electromagnetic field or on the layers of the soul must be in contact with the ground directly.

In this exercise, we will use a bowl of dirt or soil and our hands instead of our feet; this will make it easier to work indoors. We will also use the element of water to increase the magnetism of the field and attract more of the new elements.

1. The Electromagnetic Field

Exercise 4: Exercise to reset and increase the frequency of the electromagnetic field

To begin, you will need the following materials:

- A bowl of water

- A cord — a shoelace works

- A bowl of dirt or soil

Gather your materials and put them all in front of you on a table or other surface.

Now, please find a comfortable, seated position. Proceed to put your index finger of one hand in the bowl of water and the index of the other hand in the bowl of dirt. Now, let's begin to generate some electrical charge by remembering events that are positive—really important, meaningful memories that made you happy at some point in your life. This process produces an electric charge that is what we are looking to activate, reset, and intensify.

Keep these memories and emotions in your mind for one minute while the electrical circuit completes a full circle. Now grab the cord, holding one end in each han and pull both ends in opposite directions to create tension. Do this ten times to expand the intensity of the electromagnetic field. Every time that you pull the ends of the cord, you create tension and the electromagnetic field expands.

Keep the positive memories active at all times.

You should practice this exercise three to four times in a day and then leave it for a week. When you work with anything that has to do with the electricity, fire, or activation, you have to do it in an intense, continuous way to keep the momentum, emulating the nature of fire. Things that have to do with magnetism or water can be longer or more spaced.

This is a great way to raise the frequency of the field in a very gentle way, using the electric charge of your own memories. It is important that you use memories instead of thoughts, as they come from different places and have completely different effects.

Most likely your soul has created substitute emotions for those positive core emotions after you experienced them, especially if they were significant, and placed them in the emotional body of the soul. This produces an electric charge every time that you activate them.

Visualize the electricity of these memories traveling in a circular way, from the water to the earth, or dirt, which grounds it. When the cycle is stopped by the act of grounding, it forces new elements to adhere to the field to immediately fill up the void. Once these new elements start populating the field, they push out the lower frequency elements, as that is the natural response of elements of higher vs. lower frequency.

Exercise 5:
Exercise to increase the range of expansion of the electromagnetic field

Now, let's work with another exercise that will increase the range of expansion of the electromagnetic field, after the new elements have been integrated.

Again, take a bowl of water, a bowl of dirt, and a piece of a lime for this visualization. This time we will trigger some other processes in the brain by taking a few drops of lime juice. This activates the brain and stimulates numerous elements within the field.

Immediately after, place one of your hands in the water and the other one in the bowl of dirt, only your index fingers would be sufficient, and wait for one minute for a full electrical circuit to be completed.

The effect of the earthing or grounding, in the way that we are doing it here, is to discharge something from its present electric charge and ground it. In this case, we are grounding our lower level brain impulses and energy field stimuli so that we can connect to higher level ones.

We become like a battery, negative charge on one side, grounding, and positive charge on the other, which feeds our electromagnetic field.

This should only be practiced following the previous exercise, to make sure that what you are expanding are the new elements. Practice it anytime that you practice the previous exercise, but never on its own. This is a sequence.

2. The Forming Body

The first layer of the soul, from the outside to the inside, is the forming body.

The way we purge the forming body is through the same technique that we just practiced because it's composed by electromagnetic elements, but also by elements of the emotional body. The forming body doesn't store information other than what is related to processes of the soul's interaction with the electromagnetic field or with the emotional body.

The only recorded processes are usually those of purging, dissolving, or recirculating elements that could be useful to either layer. It prevents us from losing elements that we are meant to keep within the soul and promotes a healthy soul environment by letting go of or dissolving the elements that could be potentially harmful or simply unnecessary.

This layer is also responsible for deciding which elements of the emotions are ready to be released, and which should be kept as substitutes. If you have ever been through a traumatic situation and all of a sudden can't remember much of it, or anything at all, it is because the forming body made the determination that those elements were so harmful they had to be eliminated of the soul.

That doesn't mean that these elements are destroyed, as nothing can really be destroyed. They are removed from the soul and placed in the etheric space, where all things go. The etheric space is mental; it is the spatial component of the creator's mind. Everything is created by the mind and goes back to the mind.

This is the reason why, in very specific states of brain activity, usually during guided hypnosis, you may be able to reach this information again.

One thing to be said about accessing negative or traumatic memories is that if the soul made the determination that these elements were harmful for you, and for that reason they were eliminated from your immediate reach. The chances that you could cause irreparable damage if you attempt to revive them out of curiosity are high. These practices of hypnosis and psychotherapy should only be performed by professionals, and even then, they are potentially risky. My personal preference when working with people with PTSD or traumatic memories in general is, again, not to focus on what is wrong but rather focus on a state of being in which everything is in perfect order.

This is what we are targeting with this practice; by purging the layers of the soul in this way we bring awareness to our purest form. Usually a psychotherapist will guide you through the memory of these emotions to visualize them in order to release them. Instead, we are attracting the electric charge of these memories, emotions, or thoughts to then release them from the body and soul by following both an electrical discharge process and a visualization of healing the entire layer of the soul, without necessarily knowing exactly what is being removed. We reset the entire soul, layer by layer.

The way that we heal the part of this layer that is not electromagnetic, but that contains elements of the emotional body, is addressed when we the reset the emotional body

3. *The Emotional Body*

Exercise 6:
Releasing stagnated elements of the emotional body

This This exercise takes us into a state of brain activity in which we can connect with the emotional body to give it a *general release command*. After this, we will proceed to visualize the release of emotions.

This time, sit in a comfortable position and let your body relax. You will proceed to read a passage composed of paradoxes, which, when read together without interruption, create the perfect brain vibration to communicate with the layers of the soul, especially the emotional body.

Take a deep breath and carefully read the passage below without missing anything. If you miss a word or make a pause, simply start again until you can read it through without pauses. It takes a specific vibration of the brain to read an entire paradox without mistake or pause, even though it is short, and it keeps the brain resonating at a vibration that opens up our connection with the emotional layer. It also activates our connection with **the Universal Mind** because we are accessing the etheric plane.

After you read the passage once, read it again a second time with the eyes halfway open and then a third time with the eyes almost closed, just leaving the slightest opening for you to be able to read. This is only important because of the effect that the position of our eyelids have on the brain waves. The brain understands that closed eyelids represent a calmer state of brain activity.

"The day is the day, and the night is the night, but the day is not the day without the night and the night is not the night without the day."

This paradox in particular is especially powerful, so you may find me using it in other occasions. It connects us to higher levels of the Universal Mind. In this case, we will use this initial paradox to start the brain activity before proceeding to give the release commands. Then we will close with another paradox.

Any paradox can be used, but from my years of working with the frequency of words, I know that these in particular cause the effect that we are looking for, stimulating the brain to reach the appropriate wavelength for this practice.

Read these words without pause or break. If you don't read one of the words correctly, you must start again. Part of the exercise is to keep the attention and brain focus on the words.

"The day is the day, and the night is the night, but the day is not the day without the night and the night is not the night without the day."

This is my command and my desire, to release every element of the emotions that is harmful and obsolete, that I no longer need to run my basic processes as a human being, that I no longer need to be a human.

This is my command that I give now to the elements of the emotions, wherever they are, I order their release, I no longer need to accumulate emotions to operate in my full capacity. I no longer need to have them in my layers of the soul for anything else, I am free now of all the emotional charge. I release here today, every element of the emotions that is present in my soul now.

And it is done.

This is the day of the new day, in which the souls gather to celebrate the birth of a new being that is born from the ashes of another."

* * *

Now, please repeat the exercise a second time with your eyes halfway open; and a third time with the eyes as closed as possible but open enough to read.

After this, you will be ready visualize the entire process of emotion release.

Exercise 7: Visualization to Reset the Emotional Body

Imagine that you are an element of the emotions. You are a visitor in the emotional body of the soul, you have protective clothes, and you are inside a cell that looks like a bubble but is made of a solid material that is impossible to penetrate.

You are safely cruising through the soul, observing the multiple processes that occur there. You see elements flying in and out of it, some dissolving and merging into others, some splitting and losing their other half to the ether. Others leave the soul to never return.

There is a lot of activity. It is as if every element knew what to do and where to go, directed by frequencies that look like waves. They are placed like layers delimiting the space in which the elements can interact and do what they need to do.

There are elements of the emotions stored in lockers where they have a number, with their date of origin, and a role, such as activator, depressor, suppressor, magnifier, etc.; and a time of duration. Some are short-term emotions and others long-term.

All those roles dictate the different effects that the emotions can cause, and they are activated accordingly responding to stimuli of the brain or any other organ. Some of these can even be activated by external influences.

You decide to investigate further and approach this locker. There you can see copies of the emotions that you went through at different times in the past. They look like clips of a movie. You recognize a few of them with the date and effect that they caused in your system. You can recognize the long-term emotions that you have been holding onto, also some recent ones in the short-term section.

You also see a section farther back, separate from the rest, that looks like it is highly guarded. That is where the positive emotions are stored. Those are protected and cared for by a group of impenetrable frequencies. They can't be released because they are needed to activate vital processes in your physical body that restore health and good mental balance.

You decide to take a look at the stored emotions in the locker. There are all kinds of emotions, not only negative, but also some useless ones that you didn't even remember anymore. The emotional body stores every-thing no matter how small.

Then you decide that it is time to release all that you don't need any-more, so you look at the dates and see that some are so old that it's pointless to keep holding onto those. Many things have happened and now you are not in the same circumstances as you were when those emotions were triggered. As you open the locker doors, one by one, these emotions start flying out of their storage bins. They are etheric, so they begin to float up, going toward the forming body.

You look down and you can see the emotional body right under your feet, but these emotions can only go upward – that is the natural flow of the elements, and they get caught up by the forming body which immediately identifies them as elements of the emotions.

The forming body remembers your command of releasing these elements and allows them to pass. It lets them go through the formation layer and dissolve in the electromagnetic field to then split into millions of particles that float upward, returning to the Universal Mind, to be reused as individual elements for other processes of the mind.

Then you go back to the locker. This time, you are ready to let go of the elements of negative emotions. You spend some time here and consciously release some that you want to let go of permanently. You look at the dates and remember that these events happened, but there is no effect on you because you are in a bubble that is impenetrable. You only observe, as if you were watching previews in a movie theater.

You begin to open all of the locker's doors. Some of these emotions you can't even remember, but you know they need to go to. Nothing stays in the lockers. You go through every single door until nothing is left.

There are some lockers that seem to be hiding. They are in a dark section that you can barely see. You go there and even though you can't see, you can feel the surface of these locker doors with your hands and you free those emotions also. Until everything is gone.

You step back and watch every element in the room go up, ascending toward the forming body, and you watch the forming body letting them go freely, up to the immensity of the ether, out of your soul where they can no longer influence you.

You go back to the locker and you observe some tiny particles that look like shiny diamonds. Those are all over the space and are called drafts. They don't do anything on their own. They only work if there is something to activate. However, you decide to give them a good dose of water to keep them calm.

You grab a hose and pour water over these particles until they are completely covered. They are unable to react if they are submerged.

You know that your job is done here, and it is time to return to your full consciousness. You stop by the forming body and you thank it for the great job that it is doing and for letting go of all the emotions that you no longer need.

Then you descend to the emotional body and let it know that you are thankful for the job it has done your entire life, keeping good record of your emotions, but that from now on, you want to release every negative and unnecessary emotion directly to the ether. There is no need to store them anymore. And you leave, knowing that your message was understood by all the elements.

It is time to come back and continue with your life, knowing that every emotion was released, that anything that is left in the emotional body is only positive, and that you have the control to choose from now on what to let inside you, in any capacity.

Now gently stretch your feet and hands, move slowly from side to side to activate your body. Feel your head, your heart, your stomach, your legs. Welcome back.

4. The Psychosomatic Body

The next layer to reset is the psychosomatic body. It is called psychosomatic because it has to do with stimulus and response in connection with the emotional and the mental body. This layer, just like the forming body, does not store elements, but serves as a sort of distributor and organizer of elements for the mental and emotional bodies.

The way that we restructure this layer is by resetting the elements that act as boundaries between the layer itself and the mental and emotional bodies.

Those elements respond to impulses of either kind: emotional impulses, such as memories, and mental impulses, such as thoughts. We are going to activate the elements of each kind and reset them in sequence.

Exercise 8: Exercise to reset the psychosomatic body

To start please grab a bowl of water and another with your preferred earth grounding agent, dirt or soil. Thoughts and memories have electric charges that activate while these processes are running. In this exercise, we are going to run the electric cycle that the thought or memory produces and ground it in the earth as we have done before, to flush out any element that may be left in either layer.

For this we are going to work with the positive emotions that are still left in the emotional body, which won't release the positive emotions, but rather activate the electricity that runs on the psychosomatic body to allow us to reset it.

You will start by remembering the most remarkable positive memory in your life so far and revive it as if it were happening now, reactivating the emotions that you felt in that moment. Now, immediately put one hand in the bowl of water and the other one in the bowl of dirt.

Maintain this memory and the emotions for one minute approximately for the electric cycle to complete a full circuit.

Please repeat this practice three times in total and then rest. You can use the same emotion or switch to others if you like. The release of electric charge that activates the process is the same, although the charge of the elements in each memory may be different.

Once you have completed this exercise with a memory or memories, please do the same with a positive thought or any thought, as long as it's a thought that you have had before. A recurring thought or any second-hand thought would work.

Choose a situation that has not happened, something that is not a memory, only a thought.

Immediately put one hand in the bowl of water and the one in the bowl of dirt. Maintain this thought for one minute while the electric charge tries to complete a full cycle.

Repeat this practice three times and rest. Just as before, you can use the same thought, or any thought, since we are resetting the entire layer. We only care about the electric charge of the process in and of itself, not about the elements of each thought.

However, since we are working with a layer that doesn't store elements but that processes them, we will use a previously processed thought in order to reset the boundaries with the mental body, which is what stores them.

These exercises help tremendously to reset the energetic charge of the layers of the soul. You are consciously releasing elements with an action that is both etheric and physical, through the visualization and actual representation of an electric circuit. Thoughts, emotions, and memories are all etheric until they are expressed in the physical reality in the form of an action.

Storage of emotions, blockages, and all kinds of filters placed on the soul are processes that occur in relation to the lower consciousness of our elements. Once we elevate our consciousness to the next level or round of elevation, our elements change the way they react to impulses, and no longer have a need for storing emotions or thoughts to activate sensorial experiences. This is because the brain, which is the main activator of sensorial perceptions, is no longer in charge of stimulating our body and soul functions. With DNA activation we make a transition to the heart center as our main intelligence and the brain executes what this center commands, not the other way around.

In the higher levels of consciousness, the satisfaction of sensorial experiences is not on the list of basic needs. It is, on the other hand, under control and restricted to avoid imbalances.

When seen from a lower consciousness stand point, this may sound like something you won't want to do, but as soon as you have your first experiences of awareness, elevated consciousness, and sense of interconnectedness, you will want to continue elevating your consciousness and unlocking your true potential more than you will care for satisfying temporary sensorial needs. It will be a natural transition.

When we are in a higher level of consciousness, we have many more chances to respond to situations in the way that is most beneficial for us. It is almost as if we had a full perception of all the possible outcomes, and we choose to react in a way that we know will bring the best result, as opposed to simply reacting without having any clue about the consequences of our actions.

When you transfer your center of intelligence from the brain to the heart, it is as if your entire being is now intelligent, and you don't need to think to reach the best discernment or action, you simply have to allow yourself to manifest it, as the entire conglomerate of elements that is you, is attracted toward the highest consciousness solution—one that resonates with your new level of consciousness.

5. *The Mental Body*

Now we can move on to the mental body. It's necessary to work in this order because the closer to the physical body that we get, the denser the layer and its elements become. By us releasing the elements of the exterior layers first, we make the path for the other elements much lighter and accessible.

When we reach a specific vibration in the brain, also called brain waves, we can connect to various spaces of the Universal Mind, where we can find bulk ideas, thoughts, past life imprints, and other mental elements that we may or may not understand consciously from this perception of reality.

Once we connect to the mind, we can record in our mental layer a copy of the elements that we need for future use. We can classify these elements as original ideas, structured ideas, or residual ideas.

Original ideas are all those that we find in the Mind of God, or the Universal Mind, without alterations or additions from an observer. These are ideas in their pure form, without going through any filter of perception, and without acquiring any of the identifiers of the specific reality of the observer or user.

Structured Ideas are those that already went through the filters of the observer or user, adjusting the original idea for manifestation or understanding in a specific reality. Not all ideas get to be manifested in a tangible manner, but they all go through the process of restructuring unless you learn to observe original ideas without trying to adjust them to fit a specific reality.

Observing the original idea of everything is a beautiful practice, similar to what we did to recognize the original idea of the true self. It can be done in meditation at first, and then practiced regularly until it becomes your regular means of perceiving ideas.

Structured ideas are stored in the mental body for future use and can be dissected into more basic elements to use individually or in combination with elements of other structured ideas.

These can be released whenever we want. We can let go of an entire structured idea or only of some of their individual elements.

In higher levels of consciousness, we observe and interact with original ideas and only structure ideas needed to be functional in the physical reality, while still understanding their original aspects. The lesser the accumulation of structured ideas, the better the functioning of the mental layer. This helps you improve and expedite the quality of your mental processes by not being tangled up in unnecessary background processes running all at the same time when an idea is activated or perceived.

The release of structured ideas is the goal for our next exercise. This will help us to reset the mental layer.

Residual ideas are the leftover elements of structured ideas that were already released from the layer. We keep what we selectively choose to believe in and that ends up creating a new stand-alone idea deprived from its original context, which manages to activate processes and command actions on its own.

These residual ideas also need to be released to prevent interference with our awareness of the original ideas.

Everything that is in the mental layer acts as a filter of perception that affects any new idea or process that enters the layer. Once a new element enters the layer, it is stored there and merges with all the other elements in the layer, forming together what we know as our ideologies, point of view, or perspective.

The cleaner this layer is, the more objective our perception is, which means the closer we are to the original idea of that circumstance, person, or thing.

The process of accumulation of elements in the mental layer is similar to that of the emotions in the emotional layer in that we have to find the point of zero ideologies to avoid triggering any filters when a new idea enters the layer.

The natural consequence of an elevated state of consciousness is to no longer need to structure and accumulate ideas, and to instead always interact with them in their original state. This is a skill to be developed at first, but as we elevate our consciousness, it becomes an effortless thing, an intrinsic consequence of a higher perception of reality.

To release these elements, we need bring to our awareness the state of zero ideologies, a state of being before anything was established as a belief. These beliefs are not only about concepts but also about how processes in the body and soul should function. Once these are released, we can allow the new structure of the soul to establish new, more efficient processes and elements.

To return to the point of zero ideologies, we will try to remember our very first thoughts, even if you can't really remember them now, simply try to bring that moment to awareness. For that, I have lined up a series of incomplete phrases; please try to complete them with the first thought that comes to mind.

Exercise 9: Exercise to stimulate the mental body

In this exercise, you will have both of your hands in the water bowl. We are not trying to release an electric charge. In this case, we want to magnify our awareness of this state of mind. The element of water will help attract the elements of that original state of mind.

To start, please sit in a comfortable position, take a deep breath, relax the body, and put both of your hands into the water.

Now, let's begin to activate the electric charge of the mental body running through the original thought processes. I am going to provide some incomplete sentences that you will try to complete. Keep your hands in the water while you complete the sentences.

1. The day that I was born my first thought was . . .
2. The day that I was born my favorite color was . . .
3. The day that I was born my favorite person was . . .
4. The day that I was born I had many friends in the same room, and their names were . . .
5. The day that I was born my mother brought to the hospital a change of clothes, some slippers and . . .

Now you can rest for approximately ten minutes and then try it again with a new set of sentences:

1. The day that I was born my hair was . . .
2. The day that I was born I was hungry and . . .
3. The day that I was born there were people in the room that were not my relatives, they were . . .
4. The day that I was born the temperature in the room felt . . .
5. The day that I was born my mother held me tight and said . . .

Now it's time to rest for ten minutes and then repeat the exercise one last time:

1. The day that I was born my power of understanding was limited by

my experience, but I still managed to understand some things like . . .

2. The day that I was born my mother gave me a name and last name that I didn't learn until I was . . .

3. The day that I was born my family gathered to greet me and said to me . . .

4. The day that I was born I felt so confused that I didn't know if I should cry or laugh because . . .

5. The day that I was born the moment that I remember with most joy is . . .

That's all. Now you can rest.

You don't need to do this again, unless you feel that it is necessary because there is clutter in the mental layer, such as many repetitive thoughts or constant reminders.

One thing to be said about our soul, body, and spirit, is that they are immediately affected by anything that we eat. If we feed our systems foods that don't promote balance, health, and nutrition, our elements will be out of control, causing complete chaos.

One sure thing that will activate repetitive thoughts and constant brain impulses without any cause is sugar in any of its forms: processed, non-processed, stevia, or honey. The addictiveness that it produces is not dependent on the source but on the effect that it causes on the brain and the sensorial perception.

It is very important that we make an effort to keep a conscious diet that promotes balance. After elevation of consciousness, this no longer requires too much effort, it is a consequence of it, and part of the new perception of reality of the higher levels of consciousness in which we are very aware of nourishing the body, and of the pain or suffering that any other beings may go through to fulfill our needs. We can obtain the same or better results of nourishment from a plant-based diet, therefore there is no rea-son why not to go with that option instead.

In book two of this series, *The Power of the Elevation of Consciousness: Cellular Activation*, we go over changing the chemistry of the body with the establishment of a thorough food plan and exercise regimen to pro-mote the activation and reproduction of good cells and to maintain balance at all times – a necessary requirement for the process of elevation of consciousness.

However, in this book, I would like to only bring awareness to the relationship between what we eat the entire process of elevation of con-sciousness. We can complement our soul restructuring by eating foods that promote cleaning, releasing, and detoxing. We can also practice fasting to help us get rid of old, stagnated elements much faster.

Exercise 10: Releasing the elements of the mental body to reach the "zero" state

The zero state simply calls for us to be ourselves in the truest sense, using our elements and processes in the way they are meant to be used and not accumulating any beliefs, emotions, or judgements of any kind that would change the original idea of any of these processes in our body or soul.

If you really analyze this concept, it makes sense that we would want to do this, and yet our fears and insecurities (elements of the lower levels of consciousness) try to accumulate them, and we hold onto them in our search for protection and reassurance. Many of us have the subconscious belief that higher quantity means abundance and security; this is reflected in the way that we accumulate beliefs and later on it reflects in our heath, weight, relationships, and habits.

Our goal in this practice is to reach the zero state of the mental body and allow this magnificent structure to be free and clear of all unnecessary baggage.

We will see that in higher levels of consciousness, we no longer need to go back to stored concepts or wisdom; we access the information that we need anytime we want it by simply connecting to the levels of the mind where the information is alive, in its raw form. We use it, we benefit from that information, and we don't need to store it. It's that simple.

If we all followed this way of accessing information, there would be no need for wars or debates because everyone would manage the same information, directly from the source. Problems arise when someone tries to impose a different perspective on an idea or belief, and others do the same. Then we have discrepancies.

Different perspectives are only possible when we see reality through the filters of accumulated elements. There is no reason to experience different perceptions of reality if we all have the same essence, we are all the true self, and we all can reach the same levels of the mind. The problem is that we often create structured ideas instead of observing the original ones. The following exercise will help you visualize the release of accumulated elements in the mental body from their roots.

To start, please find a comfortable position and make sure that you will not be disturbed during this exercise. If you are stopped or interrupted at any point, you ought to start from the beginning, as we are building momentum to reach a specific vibration in the brain to connect to the mental layer in order to give a release command.

This time, we will begin with a paradox that I commonly use to connect to higher levels of the Universal Mind. Please repeat the paradox and then begin your visualization immediately.

"This is the day in which I leave my body to return to the source, I leave but I return; then am I really leaving anything when I say these words? All I know is that when I leave I return and when I stay I leave."

Now please imagine that you are floating gently over your body. You are an ethereal element that is part of your soul system, an element of the mental body. You see yourself hovering about one foot above the physical body. You can see yourself moving around and causing all kinds of action on the elements of the mental body with every movement.

You have never seen something like this. There are all kinds of processes running at the same time just to do one simple thing, and you realize that even for activities that are so natural like breathing, you have belief systems in place about what kind of air is good to breathe, what breathing exercises make you calm, what kind of music lowers your breathing, and more.

And it goes on, for everything that you do there are many filters to be applied. There is so much information and so many processes running at the same time that you start to feel overwhelmed. *This can't be possible,* you exclaim, so many filters for the simplest things that you didn't even know you had recorded.

How can I alleviate the work of these elements and free up some space? you wonder. All of a sudden, an element of the psychosomatic layer comes by and takes a few of the elements of the mental body to be processed and either maintained or eliminated.

You decide to follow this element to see how it does this work. In this space, all language is telepathic, so you don't really need to speak to understand what is going on. It is mental space.

You make it to the boundary between the mental and the psychosomatic body, and you witness how these elements grab old ideas that you decided to discard and place them in cells where they are escorted all the way out of the soul.

These ideas are not allowed back in. They have different cells for different kind of ideas—some of them can come back, others are not welcome.

Then you observe other ideas whose value is indeterminate—you could take them or leave them, and it would not make any difference to you. Those are placed in a cell and are also escorted out of the soul.

You spend a few minutes observing this process. The elements of the psychosomatic layer are cleaning the space all the time. As soon as something is released, something new is allowed in, and this goes on continuously.

You wonder how tired these elements are by now, after an entire life of going back and forth, releasing elements on one side and storing elements on the other.

Then you decide to do something to help the process of releasing old ideas and mental elements, and more importantly, you decide to make cellular changes to prevent every single stimulus and perception from being stored in the mental body. You choose to keep this space clean and use these elements to help you in connecting to guidance, creativity, and discernment.

You stand in the highest point of this space, from where you can observe the entire mental body, and you see passing in front of you all of the ideas that you once had about millions of things. They all start boarding a big cell that will take them completely out of the soul. One by one, they board the cell and you start feeling less and less cluttered.

You are free of any preconceptions and judgments now and you can experience any situation and perceive each thing for what it really is, in its original idea.

The cell with the old ideas and beliefs has left, and now you command the elements of the mental body that remain. From now on, their default action is to observe the original ideas of all things rather than accumulate ideas, and you do not want to judge, you want to experience the truth of all things.

The elements of the soul agree, and they let go of some extra elements that won't be necessary anymore. They also allow in new elements relating to the state of awareness in this layer, in order to allow you to be present and observe rather than creating an idea or judgment of anything that comes to you.

From now on, you know that everything that comes to you is what it is, you appreciate it and observe it, and you interact with it in its pure form. You also experience yourself for who you really are, the true self. There are no more filters that separate you from that perception.

Now it's time to return to your full expression, so you travel back to your heart center, and from there you expand back to your full physical form.

This is a way of keeping the mental body clean from any ideas, judgements, or filters that block you from experiencing awareness of original ideas. You can always meditate in this way and observe all contents of the mental body as they are released into the etheric space.

1. *The Astral Body*

The astral body is an autonomous organism that is connected to the physical body during the duration of our life as physical beings. Once the body dies, the entire soul continues existing, still powered by the spirit.

The level of consciousness that we experience when the soul separates from the physical body is the highest level of consciousness possible while still on earth. This is called New Earth, or the sixth level of consciousness.

If the elements of the soul have attained a high enough consciousness after the separation with the physical body, they are capable of regrouping and experiencing life in the astral level for as long as is needed before the spirit continues the path of elevation.

If our multidimensional elements don't experience enough elevation when the physical body dies, we return to the physical form until we learn enough lessons or go through enough circumstances to reach the elevation of consciousness needed to continue the process in the spirit form.

The astral body is our closest connection to the spiritual world, as we are able to transfer our consciousness to a non-physical form while still in the body. We do this every day when we dream, or even daydream, and in deep meditation, astral projection, and other ways in which we become aware of our astral aspect, disconnecting from the identification with the physical body, even if it is for a very short period of time.

To restructure the astral body, we will use a different technique than what we have been practicing so far. Even though this layer has similar components, its function is vastly different from that of a storage system. The astral body allows us to have non-physical experiences while in the physical body. This is a way of not completely disconnecting from our spiritual aspect while we are in the physical form and triggering our curiosity for that which we can perceive but not see.

As human beings, we have been designed in such a way that we can experience life on earth in a physical form, but also experience the soul and spirit. Being human is a multidimensional experience, not only a physical one. We can reinforce our astral body by bringing awareness to it and maintaining it for prolonged periods of time.

The longer you can remain aware of the astral body, the stronger it becomes. This is in our best interest because the astral body is our immediate shield against any external influences that could be potentially harmful to the physical body, and it protects us from the influence of our own mental and emotional bodies.

Exercise 11: Awareness of the Astral Body

Let's Let's start by practicing an exercise to lower stimulation of the brain, reduce heart rate, and slow your breathing so that we have the least interference possible from the physical body, and from there, experience awareness for a few minutes, or as long as you are able to maintain it. This will recharge and strengthen the astral body.

Focus in your breathing until it becomes very quiet, almost to the point that you don't perceive it anymore. Do not fear, you won't stop breathing. In that time and space in between breaths, and in the moment that you completely ignore your breathing, you can experience awareness.

If you are doing the exercise correctly, lowering your heart rate with calm breathing and at the same time quieting the brain, you will get to a point that you may fear not breathing. It may require some practice until you let go of that fear, trusting that your body will continue this process even if you are not aware of it, just like it does during sleep.

It's in that space and time that you lose track of your physical body and can experience spiritual awareness. Try to remain in this space, in full presence, for as long as you can.

It is important that you can reach this state and that you learn to identify it. You will need to trigger it and maintain it to activate and then to expand the process of elevation of consciousness. You must practice this exercise regularly; your experience will become more and more intense every time.

Consciousness is able to travel and is what allows for synchronized experiences between the astral and the physical body. For example, when you dream, your consciousness is in the astral plane, but you can feel the sensations of what is happening to you in the dream in the physical body.

There are elements in the soul that work as connectors, making possible that double perception of reality in which we experience the astral plane but are still in awareness of the physical body. Many of the subconscious processes that occur during our sleep can be used to solve problems that we are facing in our physical reality. Important healing processes and learning experiences happen during our sleep. But if you know how to transfer your consciousness from one plane to the other, these don't need to be only subconscious processes, and for that you need to master awareness of the spirit.

These elements have the power to connect our consciousness to both realities, deactivating the awareness of the physical body when we are in the astral plane, and deactivating the awareness of the soul when we are in the physical body. Their function is very important for our spiritual realization, and we need to keep them clear of any filters or blockages that may slow down or interfere with this process.

For that, you can use the technique that you just learned of lowering your physical stimulation and controlling your breathing until you enter the state of awareness. Once you have reached it, try to remain there for a few seconds, experiencing that spiritual connection that disrupts your identification with the physical body for the time being. Then, walk with your soul, experience your consciousness moving around the space where you are, and go as far as you can, in full awareness of your surroundings as if you were perceiving them with your physical senses.

Once you become more proficient at reaching the state of awareness, you will be able to experience this out-of-body experience for much longer periods of time.

Sometimes, I am outdoors, and I want to experience something that I am enjoying in my physical body from my astral perspective, too, because the experience in the astral plane is many times more potent than the physical one, so I proceed to reach awareness first and then I let my consciousness move across the planes. By now, I can get there in a few seconds, and it only took me two or three months of practicing being in that state to be able to replicate it quickly, at any time, especially because I have significantly reduced any interference from brain stimuli to the point of imperceptible (as a result of my diet and constant soul restructuring).

You may develop your own way to get there, but in every case, it will have to do with some kind of breathing technique because breathing is our connection to the spirit. You need to pay attention to the way it feels, which is challenging because we don't experience the soul or the spirit with the physical senses, but our physical and sensorial perspective will try to translate it into something that it can identify and understand, creating a false belief of such experience.

However, with practice you will be able to perceive with your spiritual senses instead. First you need to experience awareness, and then avoid trying to explain every experience in physical-sensorial language, simply be aware and present. The need for understanding is another belief that you will release over time.

Another fact is that as soon as you prevent brain stimuli and sensorial perception of the physical body, you start connecting to the senses of the spirit, and you begin to recognize experiences from that perspective instead.

What works for me to lower the perception of the physical senses and connect to my spiritual awareness is exhaling a full breath slowly, and then focusing on very small exhales, not on the inhales, once my lungs feel almost empty. I continue this rhythm for a few minutes until it becomes stable, and then I let it continue on its own. Then I can focus on experiencing my true self. That is when my meditation starts. At this point I can begin walking with the soul, solving a problem, attracting a person, or doing anything else I need to do.

You can develop your expertise in reaching a state of awareness even further and learn to do this while you walk or do any other activity, instead of being in deep meditation. This way you will find much easier to switch from one state to the other in a matter of seconds.

I often take my dogs for a walk on the beach, and we have such a good time that I like experiencing it in the astral plane, too, so as we walk, I also walk in awareness of my astral body. My connector elements in the astral body recognize that this is what I am doing, and they allow me to jump from one plane of consciousness to the other, and because of my continuous practice I can do this several times during the walk. Even if the experience lasts a few seconds in linear time, in the astral plane you still have a full experience because it is not affected by time.

We will practice this a little more during the astral projection chapter in book three of *The Power of Elevation of Consciousness: Elevation of Consciousness*, but first we need to develop this connection to the state of awareness so that it becomes as easy as breathing or other normal process of your human body.

Every time you practice this, you strengthen those connector elements and the entire soul, releasing fear, filters, or blockages that might be preventing you from accessing awareness. It is a natural human ability. We are given several expressions of being for a reason but chose to use only one because our level of consciousness tells us that only "I" exist, only the physical body is real, but as you reach higher levels of consciousness, you begin to realize your multidimensionality, and you are able to use your other forms of expression in any way that you wish. It is all your body!

Important note:

To document your progress and keep track of all your exercises, you can use the workbook at the end of this book or create a schedule in which to incorporate your weekly practice. Include a daily practice of awareness followed by the OBE (out of body experience). Please keep in mind that this OBE and all the practices that we are learning in this book are customized to help you reach DNA activation.

If you have other ways of executing these methods, please refrain from using those ways during the time you are practicing these teachings. Let go of old ideas and conditioning thoughts, and simply follow your practice the way it is indicated in this book.

The same goes for all other methods of releasing emotions and blockages, or of working with any of the elements mentioned in this book. To not interfere with the results of this process, please do not combine this practice with any others. If you have to perform a healing for someone else that involves sound, light, or any other vibratory therapy, afterward, please practice the initial exercises again to reset the electromagnetic field and bring awareness to the spirit. You will need to rebalance your elements to return to your optimal form.

In this schedule, you can also include your meal plan to make sure you are prepared and always have the right kind of foods handy. Failure starts when we are not prepared and end up feeding the body with something that stimulates brain impulses and obstructs awareness..

CHAPTER 3

The Multidimensional Self

Section 1: *Our Multidimensional Nature*

We are multidimensional beings, and we experience the same processes from multiple dimensional perspectives. If we have a happy circumstance, the physical body will experience it through the senses, the soul, the astral body, and the spirit in different ways.

Our consciousness is only limited to the physical experience in its lower levels, but once you ascend to higher levels of consciousness, you can experience multidimensionality, and that is when your perspective changes from "I" to "we" to "all". This doesn't mean that this event is not being registered in those dimensions already; it only means that in the lower levels of consciousness we can't perceive them.

Life for each one of us is only what we can perceive. If you expand your perception of reality, life becomes a broader, multidimensional, more comprehensive experience, but this is only possible through elevation of consciousness that requires awareness as its first activator.

The mental body also resembles, on a microcosmic level, the Universal mind, as the same processes occur in each. Our reality is a parallel dimension for the Mind—each one of us living a different reality are all variables of the Universal Mind.

The Mind is omnipresent and we are parts of it, but at the same time, we are all of it. It is like saying that your hand is part of you, but it is also you. You recognize yourself in each part of your body. You don't say that your hand belongs to someone else. The same thing happens with us and the Universal Mind. We are a part and all at the same time.

It's a popular understanding that we all have individual minds, but this is only a perception. There is only mind for all, the Universal Mind. We have a mental body in the soul that stores information that we extract from it. If we have an idea, it's not that we had the idea really. What we did was connect to the Universal Mind, where all the ideas coexist, and extract from it what we needed to store it in the mental body.

This is similar to having a virtual server to which we connect to extract the information that we need and then store it in our local hard drives.

The reason why there's multidimensionality is to be able to elevate the consciousness of all elements in a more integral way. The most effective way of doing so is through experiencing life in various levels of consciousness and forms of expression. The Universal Mind as a whole also elevates its consciousness from the collective experience of all the parallel realities that exist within it.

The process of the elevation of consciousness is also multidimensional. From our linear perspective, it's seen as a consecutive or gradual process, but in reality, it is holographic. You can visualize it as an onion, in the center is the lower consciousness, and as we elevate our consciousness, we expand and expand outwards and that makes our perception of reality bigger and bigger.

However, in a holographic perception of reality like that of the Universal Mind, all the perceptions of reality—from low to high consciousness—exist simultaneously. The entire onion is there, layer within layer of consciousness, which grouped together form the universal consciousness. All the parallel perceptions of the reality of the same object exist at the same time. In this way, the Universal Mind completes the expression of an event or our entire life as a whole.

When our consciousness expands, we are aware of the lower consciousness as well because we have lived it, but we are no longer influenced by it. The process of elevation of consciousness also observes this spherical, layered structure: in the center we have awareness, then DNA activation, and then the activation of the stimulus of elevation of consciousness. All of these need to exist at the same time to continue expanding.

We can observe consciousness at a macro level in the constant expansion of the cosmos. If linear progression was the norm, then we would see in each galaxy all the planets and stars organized in straight lines, but everything in the universe has a center around which the other elements rotate and expand.

Following the natural flow in which things in nature progress and expand, we can identify eighteen levels of consciousness: six levels for each of the three forms of expression. There are six before incarnation, in a level in which we are mental elements, brain waves in the form of ideas, concepts, paradoxes, words, sound, music, etc. There are six more in the physical form and six in the spirit form.

Although we can experience six levels in our human form, most people only get to experience the first and second levels, and return to earth over and over to continue learning from experiences that may trigger further elevation.

The levels of consciousness of the spirit are experienced after the soul and body separate and release the spirit to continue ascending toward the godhead, so the elements can finally experience eternal life, or Nirvana.

If we gain enough elevation of consciousness in our physical form, our etheric elements can regroup after the physical body is released and gain the experience in the etheric field that is needed to continue ascending through the levels of the spirit.

Some of these higher consciousness beings that are able to regroup can decide to stay in this form for as long as needed to serve humanity, as guides and teachers to help us find the way to elevation of consciousness.

We can perceive them as higher beings, energy, elements of the elevation of consciousness, destiny, thoughts, or frequencies. They manifest in us if we allow them to.

The elements of lower consciousness go back to the process and have to experience life on earth again and again until they reach high enough elevation.

Section 2: *Elevating the Consciousness of the Elements in Your Physical Body*

After we reset the elements of the soul and rearrange its layers, we have to make sure that the connection with the physical body is also reset. There are elements that connect these two, besides the ones that connect our consciousness to the astral plane and the physical plane that we already discussed. These other elements connect the layers of the soul to the physical body to enable the immediate energetic exchange between them.

These elements are the ones that allow astral healing, a way of healing the physical body by applying energy to the astral body. This energy is received by the astral body in the astral plane and resonates in its dimensional parallel, as the physical body transfers the healing energy as needed.

You can look on your own time at the many cases and documented benefits of energy healing. I have shared many articles about this in my blog and videos at **https://healersofthelight.com**.

To work with the connectors, we have to first release any blockages or obsolete elements by intensifying our awareness of the interaction between energy and the physical body.

We can perceive energy in many ways. Let's try some basic exercises first to gain confidence, and then we can try more complex uses of energy. To start, please take a black cloth and put it on your lap or on top of a table to use it as a background, and then put your hands in front of the cloth, and facing each other, touching your fingertips together and slowly separating them. Pay close attention to the space between the fingers when they separate. You will see lines of very subtle light—that is your energy!

You can also perceive it by putting your hands in front of each other and lowering the fingers of one hand half way down, as if you were fanning the other hand, you can sense the energy moving, like a tingling sensation on the palm of your other hand. Separate them enough to make sure that you are not sensing the heat of your hand instead.

Get familiar with the way energy feels so you can sense when energy tries to interact with you. You may sense it as goosebumps, warmth, or electricity too.

Now we are going to try a more complex show of energy, in which you can observe how your energy influences another being. For this example, we will use a plant.

Exercise 12: Identifying your energy

Please find two small open containers, like two plastic cups that you can punch some holes on the bottom. Grab some cotton balls and a handful of dry beans, lentils, or corn. Write with a marker the letter "A" on one of the cups and "B" on the other.

Wet the cotton balls until they are completely soaked. Create a layer on the bottom of the container with the wet cotton and place a handful of beans, lentils, or corn on top—only enough to create a layer with the grains, then cover the beans with another layer of wet cotton and let them sit uncovered in a place where they can get some light.

Now, for the next ten days you will water both plants equally, just enough to get the cotton wet, but you will talk with love to plant A, pointing to it with your index finger and telling it that you really want it to grow big and strong. Ignore plant B. Make sure that they are separated enough so as not to get the energy on plant B. Do this three times a day, taking pictures of both plants to document their growth.

After ten days, compare them side by side. If you followed the exercise correctly, plant A will be taller than plant B. Make sure to use the same kind of grains, the same amount, and the same type of containers, and to give them the same amount of water and light so that their resources are as equal as possible.

We also experience the power of our energy when we sleep. We can sense the connection between the physical body and the astral body in how we recharge after a good night of sleep.

The next exercise is to hold a cord—it could be a shoelace or similar—then grab each side and pull, creating tension. Feel that energy transferring from side to side, traveling through the cord. The cord will vibrate for a few seconds while the energy transfer occurs. This allows you to sense how the vibration of energy feels physically so you can recognize it when working with it in other levels.

These exercises give you a direct experience of energy and allow you to perceive the connection between the physical and astral body in a very simple way. The energy that we experience when healing the astral body is the same, but charged with specific instructions and a frequency that is the most appropriate to accomplish that task, just as with the plant. You are pointing a specific energy toward something with instructions for how it should be used.

Now that you have identified energy in its raw form, you are going to use this familiarity to perceive your astral body.

Find a comfortable position and lower your breathing, as we've done before, to experience awareness. Lower all interference from body processes as much as possible and focus only on the astral body, that energy that can be felt on top your skin throughout your entire body.

Let's go by sections to make it easier for you to visualize. Focus first in the energy surrounding your left hand and slowly go up your arm, be aware of this feeling on your skin, and continue moving your focus up your arm to your head. Then go down your right shoulder, right arm, to the end of your right hand.

Now be aware of that entire section that we just activated. Be aware of how the energy feels over your skin, from your left hand to your right hand going over your head. Now feel the energy going over the skin of your face, your neck, your chest, all the way down to your waist. Stay here for a few seconds, in awareness of this sensation, honoring this interaction.

Now do the same with the rest of your body, going from the waist down to one of your legs, feeling the skin tingling, and all the way down to your foot, then down the other leg and foot until you have covered the entire body. Spend a few seconds in awareness of your energy field.

Add this exercise to your schedule. Practice it every day after your awareness and OBE exercises. This should not take you more than ten to fifteen minutes in total. However, you are welcome to make it as long of a practice as you feel comfortable with. Once the disconnected strands of DNA are activated due to your constant experience of the state of awareness these will continue triggering awareness, as long as you keep the brain stimuli under control.

You will have episodes of awareness in random situations, which means that you are receiving a DNA stimulus to activate some necessary action. It feels like an immense calm followed by a fulfilling joy and a strong feeling of peace; and a need to take a specific action. It is hard to put it into words because it is an experience of the spirit, which can't be named or described.

Section 3: *Energizing the Body*

Once you have established this connection between the astral body and your physical body, you are ready to feed it energy and elevate the consciousness of your physical elements, as well. This will allow those elements to increase their potency and effectiveness in performing their functions, to improve your overall health and immune system, and enable you to connect to higher frequencies than before, to access information or activate healing.

We can energize the body in a few different ways, via:

1. the food we eat
2. a source of light
3. a source of sound
4. a source of electromagnetism
5. telluric forces
6. meditation and visualization

The number one source of energy for the body is **the food that we eat**.

Within the options of foods that we have, there are some groups that are toxic and are the principal cause of numerous illnesses and the malfunctioning of the body and brain. These also happen to be the most powerful activators of brain stimuli and can be identified because of their addictive nature, such as sugar, animal products, alcohol, coffee, chocolate, and gluten.

If we refrain from eating these groups of foods, we can control brain stimuli and release our entire system from their powerful addictive force.

In the lower levels of consciousness, almost all of our time is dedicated to satisfying sensorial needs caused by brain stimuli, and this is mainly due to the foods we eat. Nowadays, more than ninety percent of the foods available in supermarkets, especially the processed foods, contain sugar or some form of animal product, whether meat, eggs, or dairy.

This is due to the fact that these foods cause addiction, so you are most likely to buy those products again and again.

The only way to set yourself free from living to serve these brain stimuli is to eliminate these groups of foods. Reducing your intake will only help to a degree, but even a grain of sugar will activate a brain stimulus, so your safest bet is to completely detox from these. We only eat them because we have inherited the belief from our ancestors and from society that this is not only acceptable but also wanted.

You can consult a doctor who follows a plant-based (vegan) diet if you have any health concerns. He or she can personally attest to the risks or benefits of following such diet. Asking about vegan nutrition to someone who doesn't follow that type of diet themselves would be ironic.

Once you have eliminated these toxic foods from your diet, it may take a couple of weeks for your body to adapt and release all the elements that produce brain stimuli.

You can probably start to see the pattern here from all the exercises that we have practiced so far. First, we have to clean the environment, then bring in new elements, and finally reinforce them with our full awareness to them.

While we transition to a plant-based diet, free of brain stimulants like the ones I mention above, we need to help the body detox. We can do this in a few different ways. I will only offer flexible guidelines because our bodies and conditions are all different, so you can manage yourself in the way that best suits you.

There are three basic things that can help you detox, but the way that you implement them is up to you. It's always recommended that you keep a balance, and not take any one task too far or too quickly, to make sure your transition is smooth.

The first and most helpful aid in the detox process is **fasting**. This helps us use the remainder of the toxic elements left in the body and brain much faster than if we continue eating normally. During fasting, we can choose to drink water in regular amounts or more than usual, to help releasing these elements. In some cultures, fasting is observed only during daylight hours, but there is no water consumption.

You can research different methods or simply go with what feels right. Use your awareness to decide what is the best route to follow, or you may also try a few different ways of fasting during the month. I personally like to practice it only one day a week, during the hours of daylight, since by now I am clear of food toxicity, but I do run into emotional toxicity as I am exposed to regular life. This practice helps me release that, in combination with some of the meditations and practices that I have showed you so far and others that you will learn in the next chapters of this book and in the next levels of the course of *The Power of Elevation of Consciousness.*

Another very powerful way of detoxing is **resting**. There are very important healing and restructuring processes that occur in us while we rest. We all have heard of "beauty sleep". Make sure that you are getting enough sleep.

Some changes in your diet will help tremendously to sleep better, and taking a nap in the middle of the day, especially when fasting, is a great way to maximize the detoxing process.

Another great way of detoxing is **elimination**. Eliminating as much liquid as possible cleans the blood from toxic elements. For this, you can choose to drink natural water or to add to it the peel of oranges, limes, cucumber, or other citrus fruits.

There are many more ways of detoxing that I don't mention here, so feel free to research others that may work well for you, but do not take any chemical or processed supplements to accomplish this. You will have longer lasting results by being gentle and balanced than by shocking your body with products that it can't process.

The next way of refilling our systems with energy is **through a source of light**.

This means that the body can feed off the frequencies that light emits. One of the most powerful energy sources is sunlight, although nowadays there are many artificial sources of light that can produce good results. But unless we need urgent treatment for a life-threatening condition, let's stick to the natural sources.

When you expose yourself to sunlight, important healing processes are activated, and the body starts receiving the energy that the sun emits, leaving you recharged and feeling full of life. There are degrees of this sun exposure: some prefer the first rays in the morning, and to meditate or practice movement under this light to absorb as much of it as possible, while others prefer to gaze at the sunset so they end up feeling completely relaxed for the evening.

Moon exposure is different because the moon is a potent magnetic agent and may be too powerful for some people. It could cause more imbalances in our internal elements than we want. Even when we are not directly exposed to it we are affected by it regardless, so there is no need for extra exposure. In all cases, for energizing purposes, sunlight is a wonderful source available almost everywhere in the world year-round.

The next source of energy is **sound**. Now, this is something that I would like to make a remark on. Even though it is proven that sounds of certain frequencies are healthy for the body and brain, it doesn't mean that you can expose yourself to long periods of the same frequency, this could cause even more damage or imbalances.

Frequency doesn't work like that. The natural sources of energy are all intermittent, even the sun. When captured by special equipment, an intermittent sound can be identified in its emissions. Furthermore, its light is not a constant beam; it naturally oscillates, though this is not something that you can perceive because these frequencies are imperceptible to the human senses. We only perceive what we can process through the senses, but there is much more behind what we can perceive.

You must be very careful when trying to do this yourself with sound bowls or exposing yourself to some other man-made source of sound. I recommend natural sources of sound, like ocean waves, waterfalls, and even the sound of the sun and of minerals—though seemingly imperceptible, they emit sounds, too. Caves are also places with high concentrations of minerals. Spending some time in them or in nature will allow you to receive the benefits of these sounds without noticing it.

Electromagnetism is the next source of energy. We can charge our electromagnetic field, which consequently feeds our body with pure energy, with any of the exercises that we learned before. This serves to reset and expand the field. We can add to that the immense power of hands. Hands carry both electric and magnetic elements. When you lay your hands on someone else, that person can receive good or bad energy, depending on what your charge is at the moment.

Going for a massage is a great way of receiving energy, in addition to the other benefits inherent in the massage, of course. Another way of absorbing energy is through long-distance or astral healing. These are applied in the astral plane that is directly connected to the soul, and then absorbed by the body. And finally, being in touch with people or places with frequencies higher than yours also helps you raise your own frequency.

Another source of energy that we can't deny is telluric forces. This refers to the centers of energy of the planet. Telluric forces are electric currents that travel underground or under the sea. Many ancient cultures recognized this and have erected monoliths and megaliths to interact with these forces and absorb their benefits.

You can visit a place where telluric forces are more present or exteriorized through these monuments, or even mountains, to connect to this force. Once there, you can meditate and connect to the energy of the place. Walking bare-foot would be excellent, as well as placing your hands directly on the ground or stones that come out of the earth.

The last source that we will mention for now is the one of our own con-nection with the universal electromagnetic field through **meditation and visualization**. For this I would like you to try a meditation to activate the ener-gy centers of the body and connect them to the center of the universe.

Exercise 13: Exercise to connect your energy centers to the center of the universe

In essence, we are always connected to the universe, however we become self-powered by our own energy field, which can keep us from absorbing all the potent energy from the universe that we could. This exercise makes you aware of that connection and enhances the absorption of energy, mak-ing your entire being stronger and healthier.

To start, find a comfortable seated position in a place where you will not be disturbed.

Once you have eliminated all external sources of distraction, please place both of your hands with the palms facing up on your lap and breathe calmly for a few minutes to relax the body.

Bring awareness to your energy field. Imagine how it moves in the form of a torus. It is like a donut with its center in the heart. The energy field of the earth and that of the entire universe also observe the same pattern of movement.

See this energy rotate, starting from the heart and expanding from there to the other two centers, going up to the crown center and coming back into the heart center, passing by the navel.

Now bring your entire consciousness to the heart center. Place both hands on top of your heart, if you like, to help with this visualization. Imagine that your entire being is standing on your heart center, from head to toe, and that your entire consciousness is in there.

Now imagine that a huge, beautiful beam of light comes to you straight from the center of the universe—not just this universe, but from the entire cosmos to your heart center. This beam of light is bright white and yellow and comes from a place that looks like the sun, but that is millions of times larger and more potent. You establish this beam of light as a permanent source of energy for your heart center, and you feed your energy field with it.

The heart center is directly connected to the organs in the middle section of the body. Although it sends out energy to the entire body, the functions of these central organs, like the lungs, thoracic cage, and throat, are tightly connected and immediately influenced by this influx of energy.

Feel how the light goes right through you and refills your heart with energy; it heals it, removing any filters, blockages, and conditioning thoughts that the heart may have. It leaves it clean and open and places a shield around it to protect it from any dangers.

Spend a few seconds here, or minutes, as you need.

Now move your consciousness to the top of your head and spend there a few seconds to become aware of your presence.

Imagine that your entire being is standing on the crown of your head, the center that gives direct energy and influences the organs of the upper section of the body, giving the brain what it needs to accomplish all its functions. Release any limiting thoughts that you may have and let yourself receive love and energy through the crown.

Now imagine that a beam of light comes from the center of the universe right to your crown center, activating it. Imagine how this powerful, bright white and yellow light comes to you in a perfectly straight line from the center of the universe, going through your entire being, connecting to the crown, heart, and navel centers, establishing a strong connection.

Feel how this energy refills your entire body, starting from the scalp, brain, neck, and spinal cord, and connecting to the heart, making that center twice as strong now. It beautifully touches every organ and limb all the way down to your feet.

Feel how warm the energy is. It feels like a subtle tingling sensation all over you, inside and out.

Now, move your consciousness to your navel. This energy center commands the organs and extremities of the lower part of your body. See how the beam of light comes from the center of the universe directly to your navel, activating that center, powering it on.

Stay there for a few minutes in awareness of this energy center and see how the light heals anything that is needed in that center and in the lower organs.

Now that the three centers are active, imagine how a powerful green light comes from your heart toward the crown and then goes out on the sides of your body, all the way down to your feet, and then up through the navel and back to the heart in the shape of a torus or donut.

You will see how this movement that started from the activation of the centers is now constant; it can't be stopped; it repeats itself over and over in this toroidal motion, powered by the energy that comes from the center of the universe right to you.

Stay in this vision for a few minutes observing the constant movement out from the heart and back into it, then slowly bring your consciousness back to your full self and open your eyes, knowing that the energy centers of your body are being powered by the energy of the center of the universe, and that you are vibrating at this frequency, too.

Exercise 14: Inverting the flow of the energy field to reset it

In this exercise, we will reset the energy field once more with a breathing technique.

Every time that you reset the field you attract newer and updated elements, releasing any obsolete or toxic elements that may be obstructing the field. Do this a couple of times a week while you are trying to activate the DNA. This will help facilitate and expedite that process.

After your DNA is active and the elevation of consciousness has already been stimulated, you only need to do this when you feel like you can use a boost of energy. In a higher level of consciousness, however, the accumulation of negative elements is significantly lower than before, and the awareness of your connection with the universal source of energy is much more active and present. You can use this method at your discretion.

You will know when your DNA is active because you will have episodes of spontaneous awareness in random places that you do not consciously provoke via meditation or visualization. Awareness will spontaneously happen when needed. You will notice a sudden change in your sensorial perception, perhaps in the form of more light; or sounds may appear farther, everything may seem slower, etc. It is a similar feeling as when you are in deep meditation – just that you are fully conscious and perhaps even moving around.

The first thing we need to do is to find a simple way of activating our energy field by bringing awareness to it, and then we reset it. For that, we can use a simple breathing technique.

Stand up with the palms of your hands together in prayer position, in front of your heart. Bring your consciousness to the heart and breathe in a constant flow, noticing how your heartbeat changes and visualizing how the energy travels from your heart up to the crown of your head in circular motion, all the way down and back up, entering the navel and back to the heart. Do this for a couple of minutes to activate the energy field.

Once the field is active, you should feel a strong heartbeat. You can now start resetting the field by introducing a couple of irregular breathes.

If you are about to exhale, inhale again, then exhale, now inhale and inhale again, then exhale.

Follow that irregular pattern for a minute or two, inhale, inhale, exhale. Inhale, exhale, exhale. Inhale, inhale, exhale...and so on, for two minutes.

Now rest. Your heartbeat and breathing will regulate themselves, reestablishing the normal flow of the field. Your energy field follows the pattern your breathing, as the lungs and heart functions are closely related.

This probably left you a little dizzy or feeling short of breath. That is normal. The elements in the field are resetting and being reorganized, and everything will be back to its normal flow in a matter of seconds.

Section 4: *Mastering the art of awareness*

Awareness is an art. It requires practice of the four ways to attain it that we learned at the beginning of this book: DNA activation, detachment, self-control, and immersion. In mastering these four pillars, we will have also mastered awareness.

For some people, it could require more dedication than for others who have been cultivating this art from previous incarnations. There are also those who have the gift of detachment already in them. It is one of the hardest skills to practice in our modern life.

As I have covered in depth in this book, detachment is not only the act of not clinging to material possessions but also to any emotions, ideas, and identifiers that define the perception of who you are.

If you have identified by now what it takes for you to reach the state of awareness, you will be able to replicate it, and if you replicate it constantly enough and sustain it for long periods of time, you will stimulate DNA activation, which will continue activating the state of awareness in a more automated way, as DNA activation contains awareness.

Then, if you can continuously stimulate, activate, and maintain DNA activation for long periods of time, you will trigger the process of the elevation of consciousness by activating the impulse of elevation of consciousness.

We need to make a distinction between the impulse of the elevation of consciousness, which is the activator of the process, and the elevation of consciousness as an actual process, which has various levels and rounds within each level. These are parts of the same concept but represent two different aspects of it. That's why the third book of the series refers to both of these in its title.

The impulse of the elevation of consciousness contains DNA activation and awareness, and once it has been triggered, it requires more of these processes to occur simultaneously to continue elevating the consciousness to higher levels. They activate each other and are needed in order to move this machine, awareness being the initiator of all.

Everything that we have learned so far is in preparation to connect to the state of awareness. We have many more chances to reach that state in a clean soul environment, free of filters and identifiers that may change our perception of our true selves.

All of this information is needed to understand what we are looking for. By now, you should have a much clearer idea of what awareness is and how to trigger it. Now, with this exercise, you will learn how to expand it to everything that is within your perception and to maintain it for as long as you can.

Exercise 15: Practicing awareness of the All

To To start, we will practice awareness including in that experience all that we can perceive with our physical eyes, and then we can move to larger environments and so on until we reach the entire "All".

In this exercise, you will be standing, to prevent you from falling asleep or getting tired. Stand up in a corner of the room or place where you are. If you are indoors, then pay close attention to everything that is in the room. If you are outdoors, do the same; pay close attention to everything that is within your range of vision.

Go one by one reviewing each thing in your space, noticing its color, texture, feel, smell; anything that helps you identify with the senses, but try not to form any opinions about it. We need to be in awareness of the original idea of each thing in the space and experience the true self in connection with each one of them, and then as a collective. Identify their physical attributes only to help you with your visualization exercise.

Now, be aware of your breathing. Slow your breathing until it is almost imperceptible. Notice how your entire body relaxes. Be aware of your feet first, and notice how relaxed they are, even though you are standing. Notice your legs, your hips, your internal organs, your stomach, your heart, your throat, your face, your jaw, your eyes, all the way to the crown of your head.

Be aware of the entire body for a moment. Feel the energy flowing. Stay here for a few minutes.

Now be aware of your astral body. Feel it on top of your skin. It feels warm, like a tingling sensation all over you. Feel how this energy field expands, how it keeps growing larger and wider, how it begins to reach the closest element that is in your range of vision.

Feel how your energy field begins to touch the energy field of that object and notice how both fields become one. They are made of the same thing; they are unified now.

Keep going further in and start feeling the presence of that object, its texture, color, size, and feel how it begins to integrate with your own elements. You are entangled by elements. It was just an optical illusion to be separate.

Now start feeling that you have acquired those attributes. This is also you now. You feel sympathy and emotion from being reunited with this element of the earth. Stay here for a few seconds, enjoying this realization of union. Now keep going and allow this unified energy field to expand toward the next thing in your range of vision.

Once you reach the next object, unify your new field with the field of the second object. Integrate them, as they are both made of the same elements, and keep going until you reach the body of the second object. Be aware of its presence and its attributes: color, height, texture. Observe how it is united to its field, the same field that you are also part of. Now integrate the attributes of the object with your own.

You have now become all these other things in one. Keep doing that with the rest of the elements in the room or in your range of vision and then spend some time in awareness of how the entire place is connected by the ether, and how everything is one.

Feel everything in the room as if it is you, because in reality, it is.

Show appreciation, as you would show for your own body and energy field. Try to maintain this awareness for as long as you can, even after you leave that space and become familiar with that feeling.

Repeat this exercise daily, even if it is for only short periods of time, to trigger awareness.

If possible, go to different kinds of environments—indoors, outdoors, in nature, in the city—and see how you feel merging with those environments. Be aware of any changes in your experience and perception when you access these same spaces again. If you are unable to move from your location, you can visualize the different environments.

The fact that we can recognize how awareness is triggered, where the impulses come from, and how to maintain it for long periods of time, is what will allow us to develop the other necessary stimuli for the elevation of consciousness. DNA activation and the stimulus of the elevation of consciousness are more complex versions of awareness. Awareness is in the core of DNA activation, and these two are in the core of the stimulus of elevation of consciousness.

It is important to dedicate the necessary time and effort to the practice of these exercises, to make changes in your diet, to keep records of your daily experiences, and to be present, as every day brings important teachings and messages that need to be documented. Praise yourself by recognizing your daily progress. Honor your connection to the Universe and realize how blessed you are to be here, now, in awareness of the self.

CHAPTER 4

Communication and Commands for the Heart Center

The heart center is our core, the source or center of our electromagnetic energy, that force that moves the entire body and soul expanding from the heart center, creating a toroidal field.

This process is represented on a physical level by the circulation of the blood, in how the heart sends the blood to the entire body, and then it comes back to be recirculated. This process is tightly related to the action of breathing. The lunges and heart work side by side to accomplish the circulation of energy in both levels, physical and etheric.

Knowing this, we can use our breathing to communicate with the heart center.

The heart is the intelligence of the soul, just like the brain is to the body. In higher levels of consciousness, we have fully migrated from receiving the commands of brain stimuli to receiving DNA stimuli, which come from the heart center. Although DNA is everywhere, in the physical and non-physical aspects of the self, the center that powers its entire flow is the heart center.

We can give special instructions and commands to the heart center through breathing. This is one of our most precious keys to connect with the immense power of the universe that is represented in a small scale by our hearts.

The next sections are dedicated to uncovering the connection to and communication with our heart center, and to migrate the processes that, until now, we only knew how to activate from the brain to the heart.

Section 1: *The energy centers*

For the purpose of this course, we will work with three energy centers instead of using the old organization in seven chakras. The New Order, or new dharma, has reorganized the way that energy flows in the cosmos, and that is reflected in our systems, as well.

A three-center system is more effective for the interaction with the new evolutionary forces.

The first one to mention is the heart center, although it is second according to its location in the body. It is important that we get used to thinking about the energy in the form of a toroidal field, like a donut-shaped flow that starts from the heart.

Our entire being is powered by the electromagnetic energy field that comes in and out of our heart center in constant motion.

This process distributes energy, nutrients, information, messages, communications, DNA impulses, and more throughout the body and soul, via blood circulation and breathing (physical) and energy flow (etheric).

This flow of energy is caused by the electric and magnetic components of the field that provoke a constant attraction and repelling movement.

The heart is intelligent and autonomous, just like the brain, and it is connected to the non-physical aspects of our being like the soul and its functions, while the brain is connected to the physical ones. The heart center is so strong that is able to keep the physical body alive even if the brain stops working.

Our needs as brain stimuli-based beings are completely different than those that we have when we migrate to a DNA impulse-based system. It is imperative that we migrate the functions of communication and action to the heart center in order develop our full potential. When we operate in the lower levels of consciousness from brain stimuli, we don't get to expand the inherent powers of either organ. It is merely a survival mode.

The entire human race has been set in this default mode for so long that we have lost our ability to use the energy centers or even have the capacity to acknowledge them.

The next center is the crown. It is located on the top center of the head and it is responsible for most processes of communication between us and the universal source. Each one of these centers can connect directly to the universe to receive energy, information, and other frequencies, but because of its proximity to the brain, the crown allows us to perceive them as direct communication.

The third center is located over the navel. This center is in charge of most functions related to nourishing the physical body and the soul. Our astral body feeds on this energy center. It is in direct communication with our digestive process, and this is one of the reasons why what we eat influences the soul.

The navel is also in direct connection with our consciousness. It allows us to switch from astral-plane to physical-plane consciousness, and again, this further explains the relationship between our diet and the ability to attain higher consciousness.

Once we have identified them, we can proceed to open and activate these centers by bringing awareness to them, as we did in the previous exercise, connecting to the source of energy of the universe. This time we will add an extra touch of giving independence, life, and autonomy to the centers, which will help us expand their capabilities without us having to give them exact instructions for how to do it, because that might be part of the problem of why they are not expanded at the moment.

Our human consciousness has limited understanding of how certain non-physical processes work. That doesn't mean that we can't receive the benefits of experiencing them, even if we don't fully understand every part of the process.

One of the goals of the creator is that each one of his creations has autonomy, which can create itself over and over to automatize its expansion. This pattern is observed throughout nature, in the entire universe. Macro and micro systems have the ability to procreate, like animals and humans do. But sometimes we forget that creation continues beyond ourselves. Our ideas and thoughts are creations, too. They can be as alive and autonomous as we are, like how parts of our body are autonomous—the brain, the heart, and the soul.

Some ideas become ethereal beings that are so powerful that they remain alive even after their creator's body dies. Other ideas are charged with so much energy that they can be perceived through the senses, like a dense object would.

All these highly developed organisms have the quality of being autonomous, but they did not necessarily start like that. Although it is difficult to recreate the moment of creation and development of all organisms, we can observe that all forms go through a process of development in which they can either use their systems at full capacity or not, and that all depends on their level of consciousness.

The autonomy of our organs is in some way under control by neurons, cells, and elements of the soul that we have previously discussed that work as connectors. When the cells in our brain, for example start to fail, disconnection can occur, and we can suffer from the acts of autonomy of that organ. The brain starts sending signals without any connection to an executable action and that dissociation is understood as a mental condition, when it really is a brain impulse issue, not related to the mental body of the soul necessarily.

This is one of the many scenarios in which understanding the distinction and separating the human mind from the brain is very important to administer an effective cure. Mental conditions can be treated in the soul, as that is where the mental body is located, but brain damage is a separate matter that can be addressed directly in the brain.

However, a properly reprogrammed organ or system, with specific commands to function in our best interest at all times, could be a great asset. We just need to learn to communicate with our elements to instruct them and inform them about our common goals, and to make sure that every element in us is following that same purpose.

Just because we can't communicate with animals or plants effectively doesn't mean that animals don't have the capacity to fully develop their systems to the extent that those systems are meant to work. For that reason, I won't say that humans are the only ones in this realm with that capacity.

What I will say is that we certainly have it, and that is why we are going through this restructuring, to change the way things work now to reach their best possible expression. In this process, we are releasing, resetting, reprogramming, removing, and replacing elements within our systems.

The energy centers are one of the systems that are being restructured, not only in their organization, but also in their functions.

Exercise 16: Exercise to give autonomy to the energy centers

What you are about to do now will give your centers the autonomy to operate in your best interests without your direct intervention. As with everything that you are learning in this book, this requires practice and repetition until the stimulation turns into activation.

In this exercise, you are going to bring awareness to the energy centers and infuse them with an intention through your breathing. This is a simple breathing exercise that only requires a few minutes of mindful practice a day, but it will leave you energized. For that reason, it is better to practice it first thing in the morning and during your active hours of the day. Don't practice it before going to sleep, unless you find it necessary, because it might keep you awake for a few more hours.

First, find a comfortable position—you can be standing, laying, or sitting. You are going to use your hands to bring awareness to each center.

Now focus on your breathing. This must be a sustained, continuous breathing that's not necessarily low or high, or fast or slow, simply steady. Breathe like this for a few seconds until you identify the perfect rhythm.

Please put your feet together and place both hands in front of your chest in prayer position. Begin by breathing in the way that you have practiced for a few minutes until all distractions and external impulses are gone.

Bring your awareness to the heart. Feel how it beats and how it powers the entire body. Now move your consciousness to that center. Imagine that your entire self is there in the middle of the heart center. You see how the energy flows in and out and how the blood circulates in and out of the heart, perfectly.

This is the center that gives energy to your entire being and you are about to give it the freedom to act in your best interests by simply giving it the command to do so. Your heart is directly connected to your breathing, so you are going to infuse your breathing with a message for your heart.

The first thing you do is to create the message that you want to transmit. It could be something like, "Dear heart, thank you for the amazing work you do powering my entire being and moving the blood and nutrients to all the organs. I want you to please continue doing this amazing work to the best of your ability and to please do any other task that you can without my asking you. Please do everything that is in my best interests, using your full potential as a physical and spiritual organ."

The heart acknowledges your message, but you want to make sure that the message is engraved, so translate the message into an intention. Translate all of the words that you said to the heart in the form of an intention. Experience for a few seconds how that message feels.

With each breathe you take, you are going to transmit that intention to the heart. Imagine the intention going in with each inhalation. Now, breathe in five times in a continuous flow, without holding the air, depositing this intention in the heart with each inhalation, visualizing how the air carries your message and it deposits it right in the heart center. Be confident that this message has been clearly transmitted and acknowledged.

Now do the same thing with the other centers. Go to your crown center first, placing one of your hands on top of your head to bring awareness to the crown. Bring your consciousness to this center, imagining that your entire being is at the crown. Feel your entire self as if you were standing at the crown center and create your message.

It could be something like this: "Dear crown center, thank you for the amazing work you do receiving information from the universe and distributing it to my entire being. I want you to please continue doing this amazing work to the best of our ability and to please do any other task you can without my asking you. Please do everything that is in my best interests, using your full potential as a physical and spiritual organ."

Your crown center acknowledges the message. Now, you translate it into the form of an intention and breathe the message into the crown five times. You are confident that the crown center is going to do everything in its power to execute tasks that are in your best interests.

Now it's time to move to the navel. Place your hands on top of the navel to help bring awareness to this center. Also bring your consciousness here as if your entire self was in the navel. Experience this presence for a few minutes.

Now acknowledge the great job this center does transforming the nutrients of the food into energy for the body and soul. It also keeps our consciousness in the plane of reality where we are, and it can help us experience spirituality and higher consciousness from the physical body if we allow it to express its full potential.

Say thank you to the navel for this amazing job and create the message of command to deposit in this center. The message could be something like, "Dear navel center, thank you for the amazing work you do keeping my consciousness in its right place, and allowing me to experience my spiritual aspects from this physical form. I want you to please continue doing this amazing work to the best of your ability and to please do any other task you can without my asking you. Please do everything that is in my best interests using your full potential as a physical and spiritual organ."

This message is received by the navel center and you proceed to also transmit it in the form of an intention through your breathing. With each inhalation your message travels right to the navel and the message is safely deposited there.

Now you can bring your consciousness back to your full self. You have complete confidence that the message was received, and the energy centers will begin to act in your best interests as you requested without any need for you to activate processes from any other kind of stimulus.

Section 2: *Expanding the heart center*

Now that your centers are active you can expand the heart center even further. It is necessary to be aware of the power of the heart, as it is the one that moves the entire energy field and stimulates the DNA, which is key for the process of the elevation of consciousness that we are trying to trigger.

The heart center also has a center that we can call core, and this core is formed by a multitude of protons, electrons, and neutrons that cause a constant explosion, emulating the processes of stars like the sun, or the centers of other galaxies that cause the movement of expansion of everything else within that galaxy.

When observed from the top it looks like a large circle with a smaller circle in the middle, just how galaxies look, but when seen in a holographic perspective we can observe the shape of a torus, which is like a donut, except that it is not static; it is in continuous movement.

This is important because great mathematical conclusions can be drawn from the relationship between geometrical forms and the form in which DNA expands, as we mentioned before, according to the golden ratio 1.1618. We may not need to develop this information for what we are trying to attain in this book, but I will set out these key points here for anyone who is curious to look into it more deeply.

The heart center also has four pivotal points that are set around its core. Each one of them acts as a magnet with positive and negative polarities that cause the constant flow of energy. The four poles have a set of meridians that connect the ends of the positive and negative charges from one pole to another, to create what we know as the electromagnetic field.

The field can have many more points of connection within it in the form of longitudinal or latitudinal lines that together maintain the energy flow of the field so that it is always active.

Every organism, no matter how small or how big, has its own energy field that observes this same structure. If this is so, then where is the heart of the earth?

It is right in the center, where constant explosion and activity occurs to keep the planet alive.

But how can the planet be alive for so long compared to us, if we have similar structures, and we are mirror images of the macrocosm at a micro level?

This is something that we hope to discover with further studies and awareness of this center of power.

What the earth can show is a large-scale version of what the heart is able to do, but we choose to only focus on what we can observe based on experiences from the lower levels of consciousness, in which the brain commands all action.

When a fetus is in formation, the heart is developed before the brain, and when our brain dies, the heart can still operate.

These are all important keys for future discussion about how important and mysterious the heart center is for us now.

There are ways in which we can bring even more awareness to the heart center to start unlocking its full potential. With what you have learned so far, you now have a clear idea of what awareness is and how it feels. You can also move your consciousness to a specific part of the body or even to other beings and spaces to be aware of their presence. You have made great progress!

Now you can use this knowledge to make the heart center your default intelligence, your new center of stimulus that before you only attributed to the chemistry of the brain. You are long past being automated. You are now in command of the elements in your body and soul.

The heart center, just like the other centers, can receive instructions and automate them if you ask it to, but it is also able to recognize when your consciousness is higher, and these processes can take a new approach.

For example, when we connect to the Universal Mind, we usually try to change the vibration of our brain waves to attain such connection. We know that the alpha waves connect us to a certain state of mind and that the delta waves connect us to an even deeper level.

But brain waves do not necessarily connect us to the Universal Mind or to alternate realities all the time. Sometimes they connect us to our own brain stimulus, revolving around stored images and thoughts. The brain does that because it is unable to reach higher levels of the mind without proper training. But when we connect to the mind from the heart, we can reach that higher connection in a much easier way.

On the other hand, the heart center has that capability of connecting to the Mind first and then producing the brain response as a result of this connection rather than the other way around. The only difference is where we deposit our awareness to trigger this process.

Connecting to the human mind or to the Universal Mind through the energy centers allows a more direct communication, without risking the intervention of filters or other triggers that go off when a frequency comes in contact with the brain.

This is an innate ability of ours that is rarely explored. It only requires awareness and practice to change the patterns of the activation of this process. There are many other unexplored abilities of the heart center, too, which we will unlock once we learn to recognize it, open it, and expand it.

We have already practiced awareness and activation of the heart center. Let's try now to open it and allow it to express its full potential.

When we talk about opening the heart, we may encounter a lot of walls. You could find yourself saying, no way am I opening my heart! I could get hurt! But what is really more hurtful—experiencing the truth for a few minutes, hours, or days, or living a lie for the rest of your life?

It is a normal reaction to want to protect ourselves from external influences or even self-inflicted pain. This mostly happens because of the capacity of the heart to perceive the real energy of emotions, thoughts, and actions, which can be too much to handle for some people. They may prefer to see an embellished perception of reality that doesn't make too much of an impression in them, so they can continue holding onto the beliefs that they have accumulated throughout their lives.

This is a habit that we develop from our early years when we are the most open and vulnerable. We begin to build walls and filters to make sure that what we perceive is the beautified version of reality. We stop perceiving the true selves in the people around us to make them fit into the perception of reality that we have created and fulfill the expectations that we have for them or their roles in our lives.

What would happen then, if you could all of a sudden see the truth? Would you be shocked? Hurt? Disappointed?

Probably, but at least you would still be able to make changes and live fully, instead of only living a percentage of the truth.

We have the opportunity now to see things the way they really are instead of perpetuating a circumstance or relationship that only brings pain and dissatisfaction. If your family life is hurtful, instead of denying it, be aware and make the decisions needed. If you are in a career path that you don't enjoy, make the change now before committing more time and effort to it. We can name hundreds of circumstances that we cover up with fear, but we don't get to experience them in their full capacity because of that fear.

Fear is the main reason for restricting the heart and it is also the reason that we want to open it—to eliminate fear.

There will be changes!

The following exercise comes with warning signs, but also with hope.

This is only one of the many ways to clear the shields around the heart, to let it open and expand. Let's move forward in an organized manner to make sure we obtain good results.

Remember, it all depends on you and your efforts to practice the exercises the way that they are described here.

A good way of dealing with heartbreak is to make the heart unbreakable, but this is only possible when you exercise the heart, making it strong. Covering it with walls only makes you unaware and weakens the heart. The truth still unfolds the way it is supposed to. It doesn't change because you don't want to see it.

Exercise 17: Exercise to open the energy centers

In this exercise, we will practice presence from the heart to help remove any blockages or shields that can be placed there, no matter how old or how deep they are. By bringing awareness to the heart, the shields have to give in. Keep in mind that these shields only obstruct your realization of the heart and your communication with it. By intentionally trying to reestablish that awareness, the patterns are reprogrammed and released.

To start, place both hands on top of your heart, this will help you focus on that center. Start breathing in a continuous way without holding in the air. Simply let it flow in and out as normal, but with your full attention on both your breathing and how your heart reacts to each breath.

By now, you may have noticed that your heartbeat is stronger and more defined. You can feel it pounding against the palm of your hand. Your heart recognizes you recognizing it. It is a beautiful realization.

The heart is intelligent and knows what you are trying to do, and receives your gesture with much joy. It is ready for your interaction and instructions.

The heart starts pounding even faster with each breath.

This is when you can establish direct communication with the heart. Try to make peace with it. Let it know that you didn't mean to keep it in the shadows, that you were trying to protect it, but in doing, so you didn't realize that you were also blinding it from seeing the truth.

Tell the heart that you are sorry for any harm that you have caused, knowingly or unknowingly, and that you are now ready to see life in its full expression.

To release the layers that cover the heart, visualize yourself peeling layer after layer, and see how the heart shines in a very powerful way, with a bright white and yellow light, like the light of the sun. It shines potently, and with every layer that you remove it shines more and more.

Remove all the layers that you can. If you cannot remove them all, it is fine since you can do it again tomorrow and continue peeling the layers until you can see the heart shining at its fullest.

Imagine that this bright light is spinning in a clockwise motion. It spins faster and faster as the light expands. Now imagine that there is another ball of light shining on the top of your head, on your crown center. This one also spins clockwise faster and faster and the light gets more intense.

Visualize how this light on the crown of your head connects to the heart center, creating a funnel in the middle, like a tornado. See how they communicate and their light gets even brighter. Now keep extending this funnel until it reaches the navel.

See how there is another bright ball of light there that spins in clockwise motion. See how it connects to that funnel of light, and how now all three centers are connected, making their light even brighter.

Stay here for a few minutes, and keep focusing on your breathing. Now you can release any filters or blockages from the other two centers as well. Tell each one of them how thankful you are for the opportunity to expand their potential to its maximum expression, and that you are ready to clear any filters or blockages that you may have placed on them, knowingly or unknowingly. Infuse your centers with love, watching them brighten more and more with every breath.

You can come back to your full consciousness now, knowing that your centers are open and free from blockages. You can now perceive things exactly the way they are. You have learned to recognize the true self, and to see the true selves in other people, things, and even situations. You don't have to worry about forming judgements because you no longer perceive others with that approach.

You want to live life to its fullest and welcome your new perception, letting go of any fear. This is how truth is, and finally, you can see it. There are no doubts; things become very clear and only you have the power to make them be anything else other than the truth.

This exercise will allow you to start communicating with your energy centers in a way that you perhaps had not experienced before. The more that you acknowledge them, the more they will acknowledge you.

Now we can practice another exercise to open the energy centers. We want to make sure this is accomplished, so we will target it from a few different directions.

Exercise 18: Exercise to open the energy centers from the physical level

In this exercise, we will learn how to open the energy centers with movement and breathing. It is a great compliment to the meditation and visualization that we did before.

To start, make sure there will be no distractions, as we will warm up to reach an optimal rhythm of breathing and heartbeat and then give the opening commands.

This is a simple exercise, in essence, yet it requires your full focus to not get distracted and to build momentum. Please grab a piece of paper or your workbook to take notes on your progress so that you can compare them to your future practices.

You can measure your heartbeat by pressing your pulse center with two fingers. You can also do it with a heart rate monitor, like a watch or something similar.

Choose whichever means you find work most effectively so that you can measure how many more beats per minute you can count as you open your heart more and more.

First, breathe through your nose, and warm up until you get to the optimal rhythm of breathing. You will recognize this point because it feels as if, all of a sudden, your airways have opened up. There is more airflow, which is possible because of the increase in the blood circulation. If you have a chronometer on your phone or watch, you can look at the time and keep a mental note of how long it took you to get there, but don't stop to take notes now. We can't stop until we have delivered our message.

Now, activate your chronometer and begin to breathe. Focus on your breathing until you feel the airways opening. Keep a steady rhythm.

Once this happens, you are in full communication with the heart. The heart has acknowledged you, and you are acknowledging it, so now you can deliver your message.

With each inhale, imagine the heart lighting up in a bright white and yellow light. Every inhale lights up the heart brighter and brighter, and with each breath, imagine that your message is being delivered, a message of relief from any blockages, of opening up to life, of expanding to your maximum potential.

Keep breathing and delivering your message for at least another minute or two. Notice how with each breath the light becomes brighter and brighter and the heart rate increases. Now is a good time to measure your heart rate and take notes.

This is a good way to keep track of your progress. The next time it will not take you as long and you may reach an even higher heart rate. It may get to its peak, in which case you may want to slow down your breathing to keep it in that zone. For this reason, a heart rate monitor is useful but not necessary. You can always identify the point at which you are out of breath and try to stay slightly below that.

Once you have delivered the message to the heart center, you can proceed to do the same with the other energy centers, though you can take a break in between to avoid dizziness.

You can measure your heart rate while working with each energy center to identify the patterns of heart rate that occur when you reach the optimal point in each exercise.

Now, every time that you inhale, imagine the energy center that you are working with lighting up more and more, and then rest.

Make note of the time it takes you to reach the optimal point, how long you were in that zone, and what your heart rate is at the end of your practice. Also note the date and the number of practice that this was, counting your work with each center as a separate one.

It is important to keep track of all the changes that you observe in your behavior, temperament, and perception within a determined period of time and between each practice. Also, keep record of a simple timeline accompanied by notes about any events that may be worth documenting.

Although you may still require some more work to do before you can stimulate the elevation of consciousness, every step that you take in that direction must be documented. You will want to make sure that you can trace your steps back to a point when you successfully triggered awareness, or one of the other activators of stimuli, so you will be able to replicate it.

We all have specific trigger points, and these exercises are wide-ranging to ensure that if you follow them, you will get to trigger those activators of stimuli at any given part of your practice. Your success will depend on how thorough and constant your practice is. In other words, you don't need to focus on the results, only on your practice. The results will be a consequence of that.

The next chapter is dedicated to understanding the definition and the power of the activators of stimuli. Remember that you can't control that which you don't know, but once you get to manage these concepts and understand their functions, you will be able to recognize what you are looking for and what you want to manifest in yourself.

CHAPTER 5

Activators of Stimuli

Activators of stimuli are all those elements that, together or separate, cause a reaction in any aspect of our being, not just on the physical body. Stimuli are different from motivations because they demand immediate action. There's an urge to act. Meanwhile motivation is a desire to act but not one that always actually triggers an action.

For example, the activator of DNA stimuli is the state of awareness, and the activator of the stimulus of the elevation of consciousness is a combination of DNA activation and awareness. There are several activators of stimuli produced by the brain that make us take action to satisfy sensory or physiological needs.

These stimuli need to have the right combination of presence, intensity, and duration to translate to activation.

In the realm of metaphysical elements, there are millions of activators of stimuli, and yet we struggle to use just one. The limitations that we think we have are only self-imposed beliefs. There are millions of activators of stimuli to unlock our human potential to levels beyond our imaginations.

However, we have to start with these because these are the most basic ones. These activators of stimulus make you an initiate, and adept in the arts of self-discovery. Once you have mastered these activators of stimuli, there are no limits for what you can unlock

- ## Activator of DNA:

This activator is the most basic one for our human understanding and spiritual development because it is triggered by the realization of our spirituality, or by the state of awareness, which is the most elemental realization that we need to have before we can continue unfolding the unlimited power of the spirit.

Awareness activates the DNA, creating an immediate need to expand that realization of who we are and executing the programs that manifest that realization of ourselves. It activates a need to act in certain direction, an urge to make changes and start doing that what is most meaningful to you. That urge is the stimulus that DNA activation produces.

When I refer to spiritual development, I am talking about awakening and expanding all those qualities that transcend our physical being and the limitations that we believe exist as a result of our identification with the physical body.

This DNA stimulus is present in all actions that pertain to our life purpose and in the various levels of execution of the programs that help us complete that purpose. It is present in the realization of the purpose, in the urge to manifest it at the physical level, in its expansion, and in its completion. Each level of development in the program is triggered by DNA activation.

When we dedicate our lives to activities that don't have to do with our life purpose but merely fulfill a mundane need or belief, we are acting in response to brain impulses.

If you analyze what goes on in the background of both processes, you will notice that to awaken DNA impulses requires no action. It requires simply being in awareness of the true self. But awakening brain impulses requires a chemical process or action.

If you stop acting and simply remain quiet, in deep awareness of the self, as a consequence you will stimulate DNA activation. Now you have the tools to reach this quiet state of mind. You need to practice all that you have learned so far from this book, and if you have followed it diligently, by now you should be able to accomplish this without too much effort.

• Activator of elevation of consciousness:

This This is an activator that encompasses both awareness and DNA activation. It's complex because it triggers both of these at the same time. Only when these are stimulated enough can we make the shift into a new perception of reality.

There is another process that we are not going to discuss in depth at this point because it is widely covered in book two of The Power of Elevation of Consciousness: Cellular Activation. This has to do with changing the chemistry of the body through diet, breathing, and movement. It creates the right environment to procure the continuous activations required for the elevation of consciousness.

The elevation of consciousness is both a stimulus and a process. When we refer to it as a stimulus, we are talking about the trigger or activator of the process. The process, however, is manifested as a life changing expanded perception of reality.

This is the result of a sustained state of awareness and simultaneous DNA activation in a high frequency cellular environment. This is only possible after the change in the chemistry of the body and activation of the cells, due to a new diet that stimulates healthy cell production centers through breathing and movement.

Maintaining this pattern for a long enough time changes the structure of the cells, making them capable of carrying the high frequency stimulus needed for the continuous elevation in the levels of consciousness.

• Activator of gamma waves in the brain:

Through meditation and observation of the changes mentioned above, we can reach a brain frequency between 25 and 100 Hz, called gamma waves, in which we connect to a very special level of the mind that also produces other cellular changes needed to continue our path of elevation. This is the same state of awareness that initially triggers DNA activation and is also present in every activation of the stimulus of the elevation of consciousness.

When we reach gamma waves, we change the chemistry of the brain, creating what is called the **unity of conscious perception**. A state of being in which duality and the perception of having multiple states of consciousness disappears. We can experience oneness.

This is only possible after we have experienced awareness of the self and are able to identify it and recreate it for long periods of time. We also need to have attained the change in our perception of reality through activation of the elevation of consciousness.

The sustained gamma wave environment is what unlocks the magnificent capacity of the brain on a whole new level. This is the frequency at which we are perfect receptors for the frequency of oneness.

This doesn't mean that at other frequencies you can't experience spirituality; it means that at this frequency you can experience God as unity or oneness, an understanding that results from this high level of perception. At other frequencies, you experience it as a separate entity, before this activation and the change in perception are triggered.

To activate the gamma waves, you have to have experienced the other two activations mentioned above and simply remain in quiet meditation, aware of the self, which contains all. By the time you get there, this should be a very familiar state of being. The more you activate these high frequency stimuli in you, the less you have to do to continue the process of elevation of consciousness.

• Activator of motionless stimulus:

This stimulus is the one of the simplest, in theory, but hardest to reach in reality, unless you approach it from a higher level of consciousness.

If you try to simply remain motionless from a lower level of consciousness, you may not last more than a few seconds until your mind starts wandering. Your body will want to move, and you will become impatient.

This is not the case once you have attained the elevation of consciousness and can remain in gamma meditation for prolonged periods of time. This motionless stimulus locks the entire body and makes it quiet and completely unresponsive, and sets the mind in a specific space.

More experienced people are dominating the fear and immediate reactions of the body when it is unable to move, so they can make this experience last as long as desired. For others, the experience may last seconds, but during that time of zero motion, or paralysis of the body, you can experience the spirit in its fullest form while you are still in the physical body.

This experience is so profound that it triggers your next level of the elevation of consciousness, in which you realize the progression of the spiritual life—what comes after physical death, the next expression of being. Keep in mind that if you don't reach this point of the elevation of consciousness of your elements, the natural progression is not to move into another form of being but to return to the physical form until elevation can be attained.

The motionless stimulus is harmless if practiced in this way. Some people may have experienced this with the use of hallucinogenic or other psychoactive drugs, which can cause a tremendous trauma to users who have not gone through the proper awareness of all other aspects of being and states of consciousness beforehand.

It can also be experienced spontaneously in our state in-between asleep and awake, or when we open our eyes during our sleep and we are conscious of the physical reality, but our body doesn't respond to our commands.

During the time that the motionless stimulus lasts, you can also experience the ether and how everything is held there and travels through it. This state could last only seconds, but that time will be sufficient to receive any information needed. The motionless state is not affected by linear time.

While in the etheric space, we can begin to understand the Creator's Mind. All the etheric space, also known as the universe, is the Mind. In this space, all thoughts and mental processes of the creator are represented by elements of the cosmos. We begin to understand how we, too, are inside the Mind.

Experiencing this firsthand changes your perception of reality again, to a whole new degree.

These four activators of stimuli are the ones that we will interact with the most during the process of elevation of consciousness. Once we have experienced the elevation of consciousness, we can work on opening to new activations of stimuli.

Section 1: *Metaphysical aspect of the activators of stimulus of DNA and elevation of consciousness*

In this section, I will describe the stimulus of DNA and the elevation of consciousness from a more metaphysical perspective, to make sure that these concepts are understood from different angles.

We have identified the stimulus that activates DNA as the state of awareness, but what transpires for this state of awareness to fully trigger DNA
activation?

In essence, there is only one awareness. The awareness of the self is
the same for all, but in its practical application, we experience various
degrees of that realization. Although the realization is the same, for some
the experience is more intense than for others, involving sensorial perception or other activations of brain stimuli like ecstasy and paralysis of the
body for the time it lasts, which could be seconds, minutes, or even hours,
for the most adept practitioners.

An activation can occur with the same effectiveness, even if we experience low intensity reactions of the activation. These continuous activations
of DNA are triggered by continuous states of awareness, every time showing a different intensity and effect.

We are activating the DNA strands that connect us to information,
processes, and guidance about how to manifest that realization of ourselves, the true self. The programs in it are only vehicles to manifest this
awareness, and the life purpose is the general title that we have chosen to
develop such programs.

The true self wants to be recognized and embodied while we are in this
form in order to free us from it and to allow us to continue our journey of
elevation of consciousness in the levels of the spirit. For this we have to
release all false beliefs about who we are.

When we come here in this physical form, deprived of the pure spiritual
experience, we tend to forget the true self; we forget how to be aware of it
and all we see is our physical body. This ignorance makes us fall into a long
cycle of death and rebirths until we can recognize the true self. Only this
realization will free us from this cycle, and allow us to continue experiencing much higher awareness, getting closer and closer to the source of all
things, the true self.

While in the lower levels of consciousness of the physical reality, the
realization of the true self opens our eyes to recognize our spiritual aspect,

that we are not a just physical body. But once we elevate our consciousness to higher levels and we experience awareness, it becomes an experience of eternity, immortality, interconnectedness, multidimensionality, and more.

While in the physical body, we can connect to the levels of consciousness of the spirit, as well. The most experienced practitioners can feel that expansion while in the physical body, but there is a potential consequence: that we may refrain from living in the physical reality altogether because the realization of the true self is so fulfilling that we may not need to continue living in the same way that we were before. It's like if we had the ability to switch our perception of reality to a completely different form.

That means that there are higher levels of consciousness that allow you to continue existing in the physical reality. These are the ones that we will study in these books of *The Power of the Elevation of Consciousness*. But that doesn't mean that we can't continue elevating our consciousness while in the body to even higher levels. It requires tremendous control of the elements of the body and mind to maintain the physical form and its perception of reality while in those higher levels of consciousness, but it can be done.

Some students of the elevation of consciousness in eastern religions have attained such high levels that they remain in deep meditation, sometimes for the rest of their lives. Others can choose to release the physical body and continue in the levels of the spirit at will. There is no limit to what can be done when you are in control of your own elements and have embodied the true self.

This could be frightening when seen as an observer, but when you are the person who experiences the true self, there is no fear to be had.

With DNA activation, we unlock many abilities and expressions of our consciousness. One of them that I personally find fascinating and is the reason why this book is possible, is called *Gnosis* or *Jnana*. With Gnosis we access universal knowledge, and in this space, we can find every truth that we seek.

This truth comes in many ways and it gets more explicit as you ascend in the levels of consciousness. The first experiences that we have of Gnosis come in the form of one's life purpose, as this is the tool that we have chosen to guide us while in the physical body to experience the realization of the self.

What you have learned here, if practiced diligently, is meant to set the propitious circumstances to allow you to experience awareness, and from there, your dedication and devotion will take you to the next level.

Awareness is not something that you do, it is something that you are. It only needs to be recognized, but all the interference between the mind and our channels of perception could sometimes become an obstacle. As you continue developing a more favorable environment for continuous awareness, you will have more intense and lasting experiences of the true self.

The true self is inside of us, and inside of everything manifested and unmanifested. At least while we still perceive the illusion of duality, we understand it as such. After this veil is lifted, however, everything becomes only one realization. In order to help you understand it from the physical reality's perspective, I will explain it assuming the body delineates a separation between us and everything else, and expands from there.

Take a look inside your body. What do you see? Blood? Veins? Cells?

This is a micro-representation of the universe in the form of a physical body.

The true self is the universe in both aspects, physical, and etheric, but what we want to realize from our perspective is that connection between our micro universe, the physical self, and the macro universe, the etheric space.

At first, we may only see it as that, a connection, but through continuous awareness, we will develop the ability of leaving behind the boundaries between them, of merging the consciousness of what is inside of us and what is outside, into one.

The realm of possibilities is infinite. You can activate your holographic DNA at any given time, by maintaining this constant awareness of the connection of your inner true self with the etheric true self, realizing your oneness with it.

In an energetic level, our other multidimensional form of expression, this connection comes from the spirit in us and goes straight up the source of life, which is the etheric true self, the Spirit. This could be also understood as a son/father relationship and is the basis of most of the religious doctrines. Devotion to the father is a way of realizing the connection to the Spirit, while recognizing the son as holy, also.

Once you become more aware, through practice and staying away from all that activates brain stimuli, which focuses on satisfying what is temporary and belongs to the ego, you can expand your perception of reality. By elevating your consciousness, you are getting closer and closer to experiencing the true self in its pure form.

For this you need to stimulate the activator of the elevation of consciousness, which will then activate the process. I have already identified awareness as a fundamental element of the process, as well as DNA activation and cellular activation, which has to do with changing the chemistry of the physical body to allow the cells to be receptors and transmitters of much higher frequencies than at lower levels of consciousness.

The state of awareness is subsequently activated by the direct experience of the spirit in our physical body. This is an internal realization, like DNA activation, but it causes the expansion of that new reality, resulting from the experience of connection and embodiment of the macrocosmic expression of the true self, followed by the elevation of consciousness, which is a change in your perspective on life. The first one is an introspective realization, and the other two are expansive, meaning that reality expands as a result of inner realization.

Section 2: *The Process of Expansion of Consciousness*

Let's take a closer look at the mechanics of the process of elevation of consciousness, just as we have identified the mechanics in processes of the soul.

By now, you should have realized that the science of the spirit is no pseudo-science, no imaginary theory. We are working with very well defined mathematics and algorithms. If something can't be measured or proven in a tangible way, it is not a problem in the science of the spirit, but of the inability of our systems to understand it.

The true self is something that doesn't need to be measured or confirmed, nor imposed upon people. All it needs is to be recognized. It wants us to recognize that we are as much the true self inside of us, as we are the true self in everything else outside of the illusory limits of the self.

What we are studying here is a way of knowing Spirit, not by measure or scientific proof, but by direct experience. The biggest goal of this book is not for me to teach you a theory or some concepts, but for you to experience awareness of yourself and unlock all the changes that come as a consequence of that.

There is a big difference between wanting to be recognized for our actions and recognizing oneself in every action of servitude to the true self, the Creator. Only by this servitude you can attain real satisfaction, and not the temporary satisfaction of the senses, but the satisfaction that comes in the form of the gift of eternity. This is where your life purpose and programs come to play a big role in your individual processes of awareness.

These programs are the most probable path to teach you what you are learning in this course of the elevation of consciousness. What that means is that now, you can use this knowledge and apply it to everything you do. You are taking control and being proactive, leaving room for the universe to put in your path programs of a much higher nature.

The satisfaction of the senses that comes from performing actions only for oneself, or for the ego, is just a way to deter you from seeking the true self. That said, it is a necessary experience for the illusion of separation to have the effect that it has; the more lost that we are, the bigger the realization of finding ourselves in awareness of the true self.

Awareness of the true self goes beyond that which we can see or perceive with our senses. Even though we have only focused on perceiving the true self in the manifested reality so far, the true self is also present in the unmanifested reality.

The unmanifested reality holds the biggest secrets of creation because that is the place that precedes creation. All that we have experienced, and that which we get to know even in our highest levels of consciousness of the earth, is manifested. Only those elements that continue the process of elevation of consciousness, after the separation of the physical body, can attain eternity by entering the level of awareness of the unmanifested.

The levels of consciousness of the spirit are also six and have an average of six rounds within each level, just like the levels of elevation of consciousness of the earth and those that come before we assume our physical form. What I want you to notice here, is how every experience in our multidimensional aspects is similar. It makes sense that we go through various forms, and it makes even more sense that the experiences in each one of those forms are parallel and comparable in structure.

It may require completing all the levels of elevation of consciousness, physical and non-physical, before you get to any understanding and awareness of the unmanifested eternal reality of the spirit. Right now, it may even sound impossible, but keep in mind that this is only a perception from your present level of consciousness. As you expand your consciousness, the perception of reality and of what is possible also expands, making these concepts more and more attainable.

Some very experienced and highly conscious beings may grasp the immensity and eternity of the spirit while still in the physical form. In general, however, the awareness of ourselves in its full capacity may never be attained. We can only have some understanding of it, but not even Spirit can understand itself completely. One of its characteristics is that it can't be fully understood or defined; and it is meant to be that way.

However, with the proximity that we gain with the search and attempt to understand it, we reach the gift of eternity. Once we have ascended enough in this form and in the spirit form after separating from the physical body, the elements that chose to ascend reach the Godhead, or divinity, and once they are there, they continue ascending in the form of elements of the Godhead to reach the unmanifested spaces of the mind of God, the space before any creation, or pure intelligence.

The Godhead is the manifestation of all divinity, and all aspects of God that make it a creator. It is the source or center from which God creates itself, and expands, by creating everything else. We could compare it to our own process of creation when we are creators, when we manifest an idea into the physical plane. Where does that idea come from? The brain? The mind? The heart? A combination of all three and even more.

The Godhead is formless. It is not subject to the limitations of the physical form, and there is no issue of division of functions within itself. It is all at once; it is holographic. If you were able to perceive yourself as holographic, you could say that the space where the process of creation occurs is your Godhead.

There are elements in the Godhead that are capable of switching the consciousness of God from the manifested to the unmanifested reality, just like what we experience with the connectors of our astral and physical bodies, allowing us to experience the consciousness of the physical reality or the etheric one.

The process of us experiencing the spirit is comparable to the process of God experiencing its own unmanifested reality. As it is above so below. There is no reason to believe that God doesn't have the experience of multidimensional consciousness. The difference is that God can move freely between those states of consciousness because He is aware of himself.

In our levels of consciousness of the earth, the elements that participate in this process of allowing us to experience a higher perception of reality, know to give us enough awareness of the Spirit as we can handle while still in the physical body, so as not to create trauma in the psyche. They are intelligent and programmed to allow more awareness according to our capacity for processing that information. That's the reason why, when you alter their function with the use of psychoactive drugs, you are subject to possible psychic trauma that may be carried on beyond your life in this body.

As much as someone could think that these elements that regulate consciousness are allowing us to expand it, it is actually all the opposite, they are suppressing our awareness of the true self, because in our pure state, the only real state not influenced by the illusion of separation and of the forms that we take to experience the spirit, we are fully aware. We are a part of the creator, aware of all our aspects manifested and unmanifested. We perceive this physical reality by a process of compression of the true self.

A portion of the eternal true self is compressed until it can perceive this reality as true, and from there, it is slowly released until it can go back to itself fully aware of its beingness, and in this moment, we are that. The spirit in us recognizes itself as the spirit in all.

This process is called the **reverse consciousness experience of the unmanifested aspects of God**. Keep in mind that the unmanifested is where the eternal aspect of self is contained because everything that is created can also be deconstructed or terminated. That which is not created, however, is eternal. The material form or manifested reality is only one aspect that we know to be true, but in the space before creation, we can experience eternity, and reaching this space is the goal of all the elements ever created.

The multidimensionality of Spirit can be referred to in two ways: from our perspective in its microcosmic representation it is the living force inside each living thing, or at its macro level, it is understood as God himself, the life in everything. But the spirit is not really a definition of God or vice versa, it only explains one of the aspects of Spirit, the one that we have experienced in awareness, and that we perceive as God. That is still an early perception of the real immensity of He. Even when trying to explain these concepts with words we fall short because "He" only explains one of the aspects of God. He is he and she, and all polarities contained in one; He is beingness.

Until we have experienced the eternity of the unmanifested, we cannot even begin to understand God, and even then, He cannot be understood. He can only be experienced.

By the time we get to this realization we will have already become He, in the expression of He that we are to experience at that particular space and time. That is the highest level of consciousness in each form and plane of reality.

And even within this space, there are other realizations to experience before we can attain the perception of reality of oneness with all that is manifested. God himself first had to become one with all that is manifested in order to realize his unmanifested aspects. This is a parallel process of what we are experiencing with the physical body (manifested reality) and the spirit (unmanifested reality). Know thyself and you will know God.

We need to be aware of all that is one with us, oneness, to begin to experience the unmanifested reality, too.

The realization of oneness that we experience in our state of awareness from the levels of consciousness of the earth, is of a manageable degree for our understanding in the physical reality, allowing us to continue experiencing life in this plane, under its rules of physics, which we believe to be true. If we were to experience oneness in the levels of the spirit while still in the physical form, we would not be able to tolerate it, and living in this plane would be simply unbearable.

Section 3: *The Nature of the elements of the human consciousness*

This section is dedicated to understanding the nature of the elements that participate in the process of the elevation of consciousness for the earth levels only.

I already explained how they are specifically assigned to each perception of reality, and level of consciousness within that reality, to allow decompression and to expose more and more of the true self.

It's important for us to have a better understanding of the nature of the elements specific to our level and form in order to interact with and activate them, and to trigger the decompression of the spirit.

These elements can be divided into three groups:

The first group is called Reticlarineidos. I have mentioned these elements in my previous work, *The Soul Reprogramming Method*, a method that I apply upon request to heal elemental imbalances and clear the body, brain, and soul in a way that allows for the activation of the DNA.

The Reticlarineidos are those etheric elements that regulate the compression of the spirit. We can loosen up these elements by the constant activation of our DNA through the sustained states of awareness, just as we have learned in this book.

When we practice transferring our consciousness from the physical plane to the astral plane and then try to merge such realities, we loosen up the tightness of these elements. We can also use other techniques, like visualization, or meditation directly focused on these elements, to help this transition.

These elements can be found in the center of the subatomic particles of the activator of the DNA. This is why the activation of the DNA only occurs after constant stimulation of those elements. The activator of the DNA, which is the same as the activator of the state of awareness, is a particle found in the center of the atoms. These are not physical elements, just like consciousness is not physical. They are both etheric.

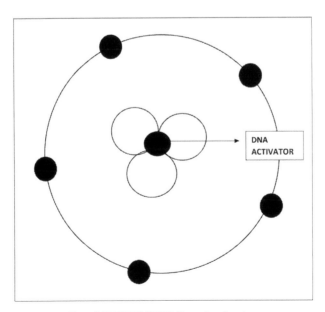

Figure 3: ACTIVATOR OF DNA. The center of an atom.

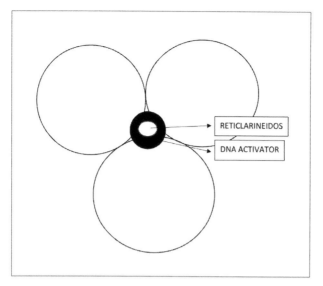

Figure 4: RETICLARINEIDOS. Nuclei of an atom.

The second group is composed by the **elements in the axis of nucleons**, which produce a force known as the strong nuclear force. This holds the particles of an atom, specifically protons and neutrons, together, surrounded by electrons, giving shape to the atom. If not for this force, the nucleons (protons and neutrons) would separate when prompted by the charge of electrons, and we would remain in frequency form.

This unification, delimited by the electrons that form the electromagnetic field is what gives us shape and form. Electrons define the form of all beings and things, giving us shape, hardness, and strength, and separating us from one another.

The electromagnetic field delimits atoms and prevents the strong nuclear force from gluing everything together. Once the physical body dies, the nuclear force is released from that aspect of being, but it remains present in our astral form.

As you can see, this process is necessary for the continuous shaping of the spirit, going from a frequency to a dense form to the spirit form. But this last form is only possible if one becomes aware of the spirit before the physical body dies. Otherwise we are condemned to innumerable cycles of death and rebirth until we can reach awareness of the spirit.

The way that we can influence nucleons to activate awareness of the spirit is by adding more negative charge to the atoms, making the atoms negative ions. Negative charge is present in the electrons, which tend to separate the nucleons, making us less aware of the illusion of density and separation. When an atom has more negative than positive electric charge, they are called negative ions.

Negative ions are abundant in clean air, especially near sources of flowing water like the ocean, rivers, waterfalls, and even our shower at home, although high levels of humidity reduce the number of negative ions present, and for that reason a cold shower would be best for a good dose of negative ions. Also, nowadays we have access to air purifiers that negatively ionize the air in enclosed spaces.

The third group is formed by the **elements in the front row between the nuclei of an atom and the orbiting electrons**. This space that is now understood as empty space, is formed by elements. They are not measurable at the moment but produce an effect of holding elements together, and at the same time, separate the particles in the atom.

Those elements in the empty space emulate the function of the most abundant substance in the universe, which keeps all the elements of the cosmos positioned in suspension and allows the orbiting of the planets and the movement of anything else in that space. It is called ether.

The structure of an atom shows at a microscopic level the same behavior of the planets orbiting around the sun.

These elements are responsible for the connection and separation of DNA stimulus in the atoms, a process that is needed for the elevation of consciousness. Once the DNA is activated, they create a seemingly static force that makes the electrons act according to a predestined stimulus and not as a separator of stimuli.

The negative charge of the atoms is what makes possible the separation of the stimulus, and their positive charge is what unites the stimulus. This continuous connection and disconnection is what constitutes the stimulus that activates DNA. This is what awareness looks like at its elemental level.

This capacity to stimulate the atoms is what differentiates us from animals, with regard to consciousness.

These three groups of elements have the capacity to regulate our consciousness and give us the illusory perception of individuality and separation. The more we learn about how to stimulate the atoms, the better we will be able to awaken our awareness of the true self. However, by the time we fully understand its process and learn to manipulate it, we will have become He.

A similar process occurs when the soul becomes aware of the spirit. By the time the soul is in full awareness of the spirit, after detaching from the physical body, it separates from the spirit and all that remains is the spirit form. Awareness of the true self means transformation in all forms of expression.

Section 4: *The Unlimited Potential of Our Senses*

As you probably have already noticed, there are parallel processes in our various forms of expression. We have senses of the body, as well as senses of the spirit, and we have access to both.

The senses of the body are so powerful that many people dedicate their entire lives to satisfying them. All of their lives are about eating, drinking, having sex, or watching other people's lives on TV. This is not a critique, just a factual statement to emphasize the power of the physical senses.

They proceed to accumulate riches just to have the means to satisfy them in the most extravagant ways possible.

The interesting thing about the physical senses is that they develop a physiological and behavioral tolerance to stimuli. Tolerance grows at very fast pace and in some cases, exceeds the capacity of any stimulus to satisfy them, taking the life out of us.

Accumulating temporary pleasures doesn't define who you are, it only takes you away from it even further. But nothing in our physical experience, not even the senses of the body, are to be despised. They need to be honored for their great value in teaching us a lesson about what is temporary and what is eternal. Without them we would not be able to experience the contrast between one and the other.

Eternity and immortality can be experienced only through the senses of the spirit, and this is what we are trying to learn to recognize with this practice.

The senses of the spirit can be summarized in the perception of one stimulus: Awareness.

Awareness sometimes is identified as ecstasy, astonishment, knowing, or awakening, but each one of these attempts to describe it only lessen its true nature. Even the word eternity can't express the real significance of that experience. We are limited by our language, and this is why in the levels of the spirit language uses no words. It only uses the transference of frequencies.

There might be some cases in which you have expressed something to someone with no words, just by the look in your eyes or the energy that you transmit. That is how telepathy travels. The more we learn how to express ourselves in this manner, the more accurate our communication will be. Words only take away from the real message.

If you want to know the real message of something you should not focus on the words themselves but in their semantics. Just like this book is written with words, but each one of them I have infused with the power of the elevation of consciousness, which is the frequency at which I was resonating when I wrote it.

The senses of the spirit can perceive the frequency in the words, but they cannot be activated by the brain. They are activated by DNA stimulus and are perceived directly in the spirit.

The spirit doesn't have a way to perceive stimuli through the physical body, but through the soul, the holographic DNA or other etheric elements like the Reticlarineidos. In energetic communication, for example, we can feel the frequency building up in the heart and then being transmitted from eye to eye.

Spiritual impulses are also sent from the heart center though the holographic DNA to one of our energetic centers in order to be decoded as a message that we can understand. This form of communication is received as intuition. When we communicate a spiritual message to someone else through frequency, the heart center prepares it to then be transmitted eye to eye.

The stimulus of awareness is perceived through the senses of the spirit, and it could be so intense, that many people spend their lives trying to replicate it, if they ever sensed it before. What they probably had not realized, however, is that there are clear mechanics behind it.

Awareness is activated by a realization of the self, and as I have mentioned before, all the components of being, body, mind, and soul, need to be cleared before we can have a true-self experience.

This is no secret but was not presented so clearly already. It was simply not the right time, however. There had to be a synchronicity with the evolutionary change for us to begin to wonder about what our true potential is, and how can we experience that while still in the physical body.

It is important to point out that the physical experience, the physical body, the senses, and all of our circumstances and relationships of the earth need to be honored, as well. It is part of the elevation of consciousness and the expansion of the perception of reality to recognize ourselves in spirit but also embrace our physical body and the experiences that we have in this form.

We need to experience this to realize our other forms of expression, but we need to do it with kindness. We must accept our own processes, the paths and family that we chose before incarnation to be our first masters, the people that came to our life in every moment of it, in need, in joy, in sadness, or in abundance. They are all masters in a way and we need to honor them all, thanking them in our hearts with appreciation for helping us be here now, in this place of realization.

The dominion of our senses, physical and spiritual, is critical to really experience the true self. In the case of the physical senses, if we learn to dominate them, we can set ourselves free from that servitude to their constant satisfaction, and by knowing their dynamics, we are able to identify when something is a brain impulse or a real-life experience. As for the spiritual senses, knowing them means knowing how to activate awareness.

The stimuli that we perceive through the senses of the spirit could have various levels of intensity, and how intense they are determines whether they are a stimulus that does or does not lead to an action, or an activator of other more complex stimuli, processes or actions; as in the case of awareness activating the DNA that is also an activator of the stimulus of the elevation of consciousness.

In some cases, awareness could act as a stimulus when we experience it without triggering DNA activation, and in other cases, it activates it, becoming part of that more complex stimulus. The same goes for the senses of the physical world. Cravings for sugar are a stimulus that makes you go eat something that contains sugar, but if this stimulus is not satisfied, it can activate another stimulus like anxiety, anger, and depression, which will command an action as well.

This doesn't mean that you should give in to the senses of the body to avoid triggering any of the other stimuli. On the contrary, you should use those opportunities to reprogram them. Using various techniques that we learned at the beginning of the book, you can tap on the organ that is producing the secondary stimulus; or you can bring forward the electric charge of a stimulus and reset it either by grounding it or by visualizing its release

CHAPTER 6

The Process of DNA Activation

I mentioned before that DNA activation comes from the stimulus of awareness, but what differentiates it from simply being awareness is that there is an action that follows it.

When the state of awareness is so powerful or is stimulated so often that it makes you take certain action, it becomes DNA activation.

This action, in general, should be one that leads to the manifestation of your life purpose, which is part of what will lead you to experience the true self in some way. This could have to do with service to others, healing yourself, or learning some specific quality that you need in order to reach your highest potential and frequency.

When we decide to come to earth, before transitioning to the physical form, we go through a selection process of the programs and circumstances that will help us elevate our consciousness to continue the path to the Godhead and beyond.

At first, we go through all the needed learning experiences in the frequency form, and when that has been completed, we enter the embryo at some given point before birth. During this gestation process, there could be several frequencies that come in and out of that embryo, experiencing different parts of the process of human evolution, until one of those decides to come to its full material expression.

The life programs that we end up living don't come with us in our frequency form. They are in that embryo, in its DNA, and we know only that the frequency of those programs is what we are looking for. We are attracted to the embryo with the resonance of these programs, and the entire environment in which that fetus is being formed.

When in the frequency form, we don't really have a clear understanding of the programs of the physical form. We only see and feel other frequencies, and that is what dictates where to go. Even after we are in the physical body, many times we don't realize what the programs are, and end up living a life that doesn't fully complete our development in the levels of consciousness, making us return as many times as needed until that is attained.

However, as we pointed out earlier, the same outcome can be completed by following the ways of the elevation of consciousness that are more appealing to you. They all lead in the same direction, and if their real essence and meaning is understood, these ways could include various spiritual practices or faiths, like the ones outlined in this book.

By taking action and attaining self-awareness, the programs could complement this realization and be in tune with it, rather than being a way of discovery. In fact, learning the path of the elevation of consciousness is a program in and of itself. The fact that you were born in this era, in which so many light workers and higher consciousness beings are needed, is also a program. Everything is interrelated to achieve a larger goal that is the elevation of consciousness in its collective aspect.

Sometimes we have preconceived notions about our careers and our purposes in life that make it very difficult to see the real purpose. Sometimes it is not a job, but simply being; our presence and existence is the purpose, and we are a living manifestation of a message of higher consciousness.

A very dear client of mine complains because her life purpose calls her to be herself, and that is the hardest thing to do for her; she is very sensitive to other people's energies, and to the energy of the circumstances that she is in. All this obstructs her awareness, so I explained to her: that which is the most difficult thing is usually the most beautiful thing, too, because it leads you to experiencing true self-awareness.

Can you imagine? Being able to face your fears instead of indefinitely ignoring them. Learning is not about being happy all the time. We also need times of deep introspective reflection, and unless you proactively seek them out, they will seek you.

But here is where our beliefs and perception of our circumstances come to play a role again. Why is introspection and being faced with our mistakes and fears a negative thing? Yes, there is some temporary discomfort, but there is an even bigger sense of accomplishment once you have moved past them.

The same doesn't occur if you simply ignore them. That just makes them stay with you anywhere you go. They become your ethereal backpack.

This happens a lot when we try to find out what our life purpose is. We have to first recognize a lack of that quality or quantity to then realize a purpose exists. Just as with the body and the spirit, to experience the spirit, you need to be in another form.

Once you have had that first experience of awareness followed by an action, then you can say you have experienced a first DNA activation, otherwise you are stimulating it but not fully activating it. You have to look at it like a car that has not been started in a very long time. At first, you push the ignition button or turn the key and nothing happens. Then the next time there is a little action, and by the third time, the car is on.

It is the same thing with DNA activation. The key is to continuously experience the state of awareness, the stimulus at some point will cause you to react, and that will be the first full activation.

The next activations of the DNA are the rest of the pieces of the puzzle. Every time that you experience it, then you can receive information about what to do next. If on the first activation, you realize that part of your life purpose to start a charitable cause and start researching about it, then with the second activation, you will know better what to do next to make it live. Then on the third try, you will know how to establish it, and so on.

We go through several DNA activations in our life. It is not something that you may experience every day, but it can often give you the push that you need.

If at some point you feel that there is something missing, and the impulses have stopped, it is because you are in the period of separation of the stimulus, which only means that one or more of your holographic DNA strands needed to separate from something that you are now. This could be something that you do, a perception you have, or a relationship, to move into something else of a higher nature.

We can observe this natural movement even in the stars that go through periods of retrograde. Sometimes it's necessary to take time to restructure, and then return to the exercise stronger.

Section 1: *Recognizing Your Life Purpose*

After having diligently worked through all the exercises of this book, you can begin to recognize your life purpose using your awareness. Keep in mind that life purpose is an expression of your being in a "doing". It is you manifested in an action, another show of our multidimensionality and the parallel processes that occur through our entire existence in any form. As it is inside, so it is out!

You just need a little practice to learn to decode what else is written in that DNA language through awareness. Every time that you have an encounter with yourself, something new is revealed. It's like when you read a good book more than once. Every time it has a new message.

Let's try it!

Exercise #19: Exercise to recognize your life purpose

For this exercise, you will need to have a pen and paper handy.

We are working from the premise that you have already experienced awareness. If you have not, I strongly suggest that you review your practice to make sure that you get to experience it before trying this, for best results.

We are also working with the original idea of the true self. When we did the exercise where you took notes about all your identifiers, there were a lot of things on that list that you thought that really described you, and you had to let go of them to find out who you were, in the true sense of being.

Let's connect again with that experience of the true self.

Start by slowing your breathing. Exhale all the air out of your lungs, and with the last bit of air, begin to take very short breathes, until all your systems start calming down.

Focus only on your exhalations until you reach a steady rhythm and your breathing becomes imperceptible.

Once you are in that space of relaxation, think about your experience of awareness, think about that feeling of being yourself, minus any of the things on that list of identifiers. No one else is there, no one can see you or hear you, and so the identifiers would not matter anyway. There are no observers; it's only you.

There is no space and no time. You are floating peacefully. Feel your body floating in the room. Everything feels so relaxed.

Now feel how you ascend to the center of the universe. There is a sun there that is millions of times brighter and bigger than the one in our galaxy. This place is called the Origin. You stand in front of it, and nothing happens to you. You are etheric. Feel the light of this immense sun touching you. It feels slightly warm, very peaceful, and very comfortable. It is something that you recognize, something that you are.

Stay here for a few minutes contemplating the Origin, and let it show you any messages that might be there for you.

What is the first thing that comes to your mind?

Are there any other people involved?

Do you recognize a location?

What are you doing?

How does it feel?

Stay here for as long as needed until you can get this information.

Now ask the origin to help you find your life purpose.

Ask for clearer answers, and simply let it be.

Thank the origin for being the central centrifugal force of the universe and for being the generator of life.

Start returning to your body. You are floating peacefully among the stars and start coming down until you enter your body again.

Begin moving your toes and fingers, your legs and arms, your neck, and when you feel ready, very gently open your eyes.

Now please write down the information that you received from the origin. If there is anything new that you experienced, you can also write it here. It could be anything – don't force it. Just let your hand move without command.

Take your time. Now, try to identify whether any of what you have could have to do with your life purpose. How does it feel to know that?

Is it a positive feeling? Scared? Nervous? Excited? Make note of this, too.

Very good! Now write down a list of five things that you love to do and also to be. This is your top 5. They could also be people, animals, or things. Don't feel forced to name people in your family out of obligation. Write the first things that come to mind that you love.

Now let's try to link that list to the other information that you wrote. How are the items related?

Is there any nexus that you may not have perceived before?

Now please also write five things that you don't like, or that you would like to change in you or in the world.

Use that information to see if that could give more structure to the conclusion about your life purpose.

The life purpose doesn't need to immediately fit into a description or a career path. It could be an internal realization, a knowing of what is next or what you need to do.

Take this information that you have gathered, and for the next five days, meditate on the global feeling that you get from combining all of this information into one idea. The answer could be laying in the semantics of the words—in the space between the words or in their meaning, and not in the words themselves.

This awareness will help you activate the elements of the programs that you have chosen to develop your life purpose, making the messages and synchronicities much clearer.

The key is not trying to give it a title at first, but simply to recognize that awareness of the purpose, to feel its frequency. Continue practicing awareness of the true self and this exercise of connecting to the origin for guidance, and every time you come back from that encounter, write down your first thoughts. This will help you develop your connection with source and your inner-self communication, and will bring you closer to finding more clues about your life purpose and programs.

Section 2: *Programs*

It is as important as everything else that we have learned in this book to understand the nature and functioning of our elements and processes, to be able to use them or transform them into something that we can use for the elevation of our consciousness.

Programs are no different. We can categorize them in three main groups.

Primary programs

The first kind are the **primary programs**. I have also called them *main* programs in some of my videos or lectures. The primary programs take priority in helping to develop your life purpose. They are the best candidates to help live out your life purpose without leaving anything behind.

It is our goal to be able to identify and execute them within our lifetime in earth. Accomplishing them will grant us the elevation of consciousness and frequency that we need in order to reach the levels of the spirit, instead of having to return once again to the physical form to keep trying to experience that realization.

However, we have also mentioned that if you chose to proactively elevate your consciousness regardless of what programs you are living now, everything that you do will adjust to your new perspective of life rather than you having to change what you are doing to trigger that new perspective.

In this case, once you change your perception of life with higher consciousness, your life purpose will also be clearer and will stand out, making you want to change some aspects of your life related the old perspective.

This coming back to earth that I have mentioned—for elements that resonate in lower levels of consciousness—means that your elements of the soul and spirit return to continue the learning process that has been initiated, possibly many lives ago. Through many incarnations, the elements of lower consciousness are split and atomized in millions of parts and spread out through other beings and elements to help them in the process of elevation, while those elements that have gained some experience are able to regroup and incarnate as a whole, together with other elements that may resonate at the same frequency but that come from other sources.

While you are alive on earth, there are also elements coming in and out of your body and soul, constantly trying to learn from your life experience, to build a program or acquire a specific frequency, and then keep going.

But you will not have access to the knowledge and abilities that you could have developed in the past unless that you activate your DNA. That is the channel that connects you to all the information in your life records and to many more sources.

On the other hand, if you attain elevation of consciousness, your elements can raise their frequency, which allows them to remain integrated or to regroup after the separation of the physical body. There is a direct effect on the DNA during this process, and as we saw before, it expands in a specific way. That expansion is another expression of our multidimensional nature. Consciousness expands, DNA expands, and our perception expands, all at the same time.

The programs that we chose are designed to be the conductors of that frequency that brings awareness. They act as containers of frequency. Once the program is in execution, the frequency starts to be released.

However, before our incarnation, we don't really know what we are getting into; we can only recognize the frequencies in that form.

At that time, it may have seemed like a good idea to choose a determined life purpose—perhaps family and certain circumstances over others—but once we are in the physical form, it is a completely different experience. This makes sense if you think about it for a moment. If you knew exactly what you were going to experience, perhaps we would all have only positive programs, and we know that this is surely not the case.

However, the result is the same: the elevation of consciousness. That frequency can be manifested in many different ways, but the goal of life in the physical form is one. Knowing this, we can hope to achieve it without worrying too much about the programs, but rather trusting that once our perspective changes, we will be able to see more clearly. All we need to do is to recognize the nature of the programs, and then we can mold them into what we want.

Secondary programs

These are all those programs that train us, prepare us, and guide us toward developing the primary programs.

For example, if your life purpose is to learn to recognize yourself, and find self-awareness, then your primary program could be positive or negative depending on your level of connectedness and how open you are to receiving messages or inner guidance. In that sense, you could learn through positive programming, intuitively guided to live programs that put you in touch with the true self, that which exalts your spirit.

That doesn't mean that if the program is self-awareness, that the experience is all about you. You can experience self-awareness through many avenues, which include detaching completely from your individuality by devoting your life to a cause, volunteering, helping others, etc. Others force you to go on an introspective life search, even by being jailed, unable to move, or sick for long periods of time.

If you love animals, for example, you could become a veterinarian or start a rescue group or a sanctuary, but if awareness has not been your strong suit, some programs that could come across at first as negative experiences start pointing you in that direction. You may begin to work at an animal shelter and have to see the terrible cases that come in, and that shocks you and makes you want to become an animal advocate. One way or another, the program unfolds. That experience is a secondary program, a preparation that leads you to the execution of the primary program.

Although we can't really say that an experience is negative if at the end you attained self-awareness, going through it could be uncomfortable, to say the least. So, their negative aspect is relative. Another way to look at them is as active or passive programming.

If you are actively developing your program, then you have control of the outcome by meeting your goals, but if you don't take action, then your programs take action for you.

In this example, the secondary programs are any events that help you to either learn the traits that you chose to actively nurture in yourself, or to put you in the situation or situations that lead to the execution of the primary program.

These secondary programs are common in our early life. If you are a parent, you can try to awaken your children's interests by presenting them with various arts and crafts that are manageable for their age. Find something that can be flexible enough for them to make it a true expression of self instead of copying a process from someone else. Activities that are open-ended, such as painting, molding, playing with very basic toys, or learning to play a musical instrument, are great ways to awaken those programs and making it easier for them to find their path later in life.

You can experience these secondary programs at any age. We are constantly learning how to better accomplish our main program, however it's likely that you had most of these experiences during childhood or adolescence, as that is the most natural time for these programs to manifest.

It is also possible that you were removed from those programs by taking the direction that others thought is better for you. Parents, societal trends, other people, and even your own choices may have led you astray based on false beliefs about yourself, but even if that is the case, now you know how to retake control.

A good way of recognizing these programs and using them as indicators of your life purpose is to go back to your childhood memories and try to remember what you stood for back then, before other influences took you in different directions.

During my entire childhood and teen years, my parents were very open to let me explore whatever I wanted. They let me go anywhere, study anything I wanted, hang out with all kinds of people, and although they offered their advice, I ultimately chose what I wanted to do. This level of independence also made me able to discern what was good for me or not, on my own, from a very young age. I didn't depend on their protection and was basically independent even as a child, and that was an invaluable experience that allowed me to live in various places, start new ventures without any fear, stand for what I believe in, and more.

They probably did it because they didn't know better. They had to work and were worried about their own lives, and they were very young, but this was the situation I chose to be born into in this physical form. Regardless of the process involved, the consequences were accomplished as planned. Although this same program could have gone in many different directions—I could have become addicted to drugs or alcohol, or I could have had all sorts of other people in my life to take care of that would have delayed or completely obstructed this very moment.

But instead, all that time alone helped me to develop my creativity and self-sustainability. I learned to sell my parents' belongings outside of the house. Then I learned the best chocolate cake recipe ever and sold cakes in elementary school during my breaks. I didn't need to—my parents have always been in a good position—but I was an entrepreneur. It was my time to learn that I could do anything I wanted, and that I would be always fine.

Once I learned that, it became boring, and I left the entrepreneurial life to pursue my interest in metaphysics and philosophy. By the age of twelve,

I had learned about past-life regressions, hypnosis, and long-distance communication.

I can now see this same pattern repeating itself in my adult life, and as you probably guessed, I am now fully prepared.

Identify your patterns. Is there something that you did in your child-hood or younger years that is repeating again?

Now identify whether that pattern is a program or a habit of conduct.

Don't worry, awareness will take care of the habits. You only need to recognize the programs..

Third-tier programs

These are all the programs that replace other programs, whether prima-ry or secondary. They offer multiple possible scenarios in addition to the other two.

If you are unable to identify the primary program and the primordial circumstances for its execution have changed, then a third-tier program comes into place. They are the default programs to allow you experience awareness and higher consciousness in a less traditional way. They are something like an emergency program, a "break the glass in case you didn't see it" type of program.

However, even with all this, sometimes we don't get to experience awareness and must go back to the cycle of life and death.

It is hard to recognize when you are living a third-tier program or one of the others because their goal is to accomplish the same experience. All we can do on our end is to try to awaken awareness and develop its constant practice to continue triggering all the other activations that come with it. All the programs lead to that, one way or another. They are just trying to help us by showing us the way to awareness through something that is more recognizable because we already have an interest or attraction to those frequencies.

This discovery is important because it means that if you are able to recognize yourself through experiencing awareness. You don't need to go through any negative programming that might be in place or scheduled to start in the future. You are in control instead of being passive about it. As a result, you experience healing, balance, and release of all negative elements that you don't need.

That leads me to comfortably say that awareness, DNA activation, and the elevation of consciousness can heal you.

Section 3: *Activating your own healing*

What you have learned so far in this book has pointed you in the right direction to attain self-healing and self-realization.

This process is not a simple one, but with constant practice, you will become more and more familiar with how to initiate and maintain awareness, and in that environment, many cellular changes occur. You are also aware that there is a continuation to this process. That is to be presented in the second book of The Power of Elevation of Consciousness: Cellular Activation, in which I address dietary changes, breathing techniques, and movement to directly engage with the physical body and cause integral change in its chemistry and in the functions of all our systems.

To see real progress, it is important to make these meditations and changes part of your daily routine. Remember that in our daily life we are influenced by millions of things that can distract us and contaminate our perception.

With every stimulation of the DNA, through awareness, we correct imperfections and imbalances and release negative elements from our soul system, the same way that we will in the next volume with the physical body. This healing is possible because being aware of the truth makes everything else that is not you false or nonexistent. This includes disease, pain, and suffering of all kinds. We know now that this is not the true self, and we can apply the same principle to the physical plane.

If you eat something that is not true food, you are feeding yourself a lie, an imbalance, a blockage. There are specific ways to detox the body, just as we did for the soul, and we only need to implement and practice a change in perception to prepare ourselves for what comes next: the expansion of life.

Reflect on this! If you can perceive the true self, once you experience it, you can't go back to believing in false and temporary things like disease or imbalance. Many people who attain self-healing through holistic healing can say that they don't believe in disease. They realized that all there is, is self-inflicted pain from clinging to false beliefs.

If every cell and every element in you knows this, they will reject that which is not true. They will try to connect to that state of balance and truth, rather than any other state that you may have been resonating in, due to your beliefs, perception of your circumstances, relationships, or energies that you were managing.

This is how energy healing works. It is the opposite of what happens in westernized medicine, in which they focus in the problem and attack it from its physical expression to stop its temporary effects. Instead, we focus on the truth, on the pure state of something, on its pure energy and inner spirit, and by maintaining that awareness, we can heal.

We don't focus on that which is false.

How many times have you heard of placebos working just as well as medicine? Doctors give their patients sugar pills, making them believe they are taking some real medicine, and they observe the same results as those who actually do. Obviously, this can't be applied to all cases, but I am specifically referring to those of regenerative nature.

How much of healing is a belief?

All of it is.

Then what if we recognize ourselves and that becomes our belief?

One that comes from your own direct experience.

I have always practiced this, since I was a child. I said I would never recognize a fever or cough as true, and as I pushed through my day, in just a few hours or even minutes, I was back to my normal self. This is one of those things that I found in my childhood about my life purpose that I am using today, together with many others that only make sense to me of course.

My parents thought that I was just pretending to feel better, so I could go out to play or eat ice cream, which was not allowed when I was sick. The truth is that I was really fine. I still do it to this day; however, I don't really need it as often. I may get a cold every four years, or when I go through something that makes me sad I could feel out of balance, but now I have the tools to fix it quickly.

The last shaking experience that my body went through was actually DNA activation several years ago. It felt like if things were changing inside of me. The first symptom was accelerated heart rate and also a feeling of getting much more oxygen, which now makes total sense because I understand that this activation comes from the heart center and is distributed to the entire body and energy field from there, thanks to the action of the heart and lungs. Back then I had fewer details. All I knew is that everything was going to be ok, and I could hear this clear voice inside of me, my inner voice, saying, you need to have blind faith. So, I agreed, and let my body go through the process.

My clairvoyance, clairaudience, and clairsentience all woke at once, as if they were just waiting for that to happen. I had always been intuitive, but this was many, many, many times stronger. I became very sensitive to the light. My eyes can sense the change in light and anything that moves that is a body of light gets my attention right away.

I went through the whole dietary change, which we will study in book two. This completely transformed my mood and balanced my hormones. I no longer experience the fight or flight reaction, or any reaction, basically.

I spent long time in self-reflection, and I also stepped into extreme asceticism, which I gradually balanced until finding the right combination of nourishment, movement, awareness, and integration in the physical reality. I had a lot of questions, and I discovered that I also had the answers. I spent a year or more not wanting to leave the house at all because what I was experiencing on my own, learning through gnosis and writing was so much better than any social experience, but I knew that the time would come when all that I had learned to date needed to be applied, or shared.

I was in constant awareness, and my DNA would activate spontaneously anywhere. I went through all the levels of elevation of consciousness until I started experiencing something very particular. I was so stimulated and so elevated in consciousness that I started losing the awareness of my physical body.

There were times when I could not see myself as a dense being. I could see through my hands as if they were transparent. This happened more than once while I was fully awake, and that scared me, to say the least. I was not 100% ready to simply vanish into the ether, or whatever it was that I was about to experience. So I decided to ground myself, choosing to remain in the physical form to be able to share this with others, knowing as I do now the way to recreate the entire process from the experience that I had lived during those years of deep reflection and constant awareness.

The part of me that was still aware of my physical self felt that there were many incomplete things, so I could not go yet. I still wanted to share more things with you all before continuing my journey through the elevation of consciousness in the spirit form, so I decided to stay for longer to share the knowledge that I gained from being at that high level of awareness and consciousness, having reached the level of separating from the physical body.

And although I was scared (who wouldn't be, if they started vanishing into the ethereal space while fully awake?), the part of me that was aware of the spirit felt very peaceful. There was no pain or worry, or thoughts about the people or things that you must leave behind. It felt like the present time at its fullest. It is like waking up from a dream. You know that the dream is not really there, that it's an illusion. It feels the same way when you start to separate from the body.

It was a very interesting experience, especially to be able to experience the contrast in both forms of expression.

It is definitely not the same as an out-of-body experience because in those instances, you have some certainty that you will return. It is a completely different feeling that is also not a feeling, because we don't have access to our physical senses. It is more like a knowing and being.

This is what prompted me to write these books, which are divided in three parts because they are all equally important for the elevation of consciousness, and I decided to honor them as parallel processes. You need to find that multidimensional expression in everything you do and are, and to realize when you are in front of a parallel expression of that doing or being.

Unfortunately, our physical-plane perception does not allow us to experience the holographic perspective. If that were the case, we would be experiencing all three levels at once. Since we are still in a linear time perception, we have to see things in stages.

Keep in mind that since we are working with stimulus and activation, it is important to keep the momentum going, keep practicing, and move on to the next level. Then once you have gone through all of the theory and practice, try to make that experience holographic by integrating all that you have learned into one moment.

The best way to do that is simply by experiencing awareness, and your new perception of life at each level of consciousness will take care of integrating everything into one.

Until the next volume.

> With infinite love,
> Johanna Bassols.

Workbook

This workbook is a supplement for the book or online classes of book 1 of *The Power of Elevation of Consciousness: Soul Restructuring.*

Here you can keep track of your progress for each one of the exercises in the book.

Keep in mind that the goal of this practice is to accomplish an activation of your enhanced awareness and holographic DNA. For best results you need to stimulate awareness in a constant and intense way, in the shortest time possible. Once you start, make a commitment to complete all the exercises within a reasonable time frame.

You can practice the exercise first and then determine how long it took you, and then determine when you can schedule it to practice again.

Not all exercises need to be practiced continuously. Some of them, like the ones to reset the electromagnetic field or the layers of the soul are only needed from time to time. Others, like the exercises to practice awareness should be part of your regular practice.

Incorporating the state of awareness into everything you do, is a better way to experience than making this an isolated event a few times a week. However, at the beginning, this is necessary for you to learn to identify awareness. Then you can make this part of your new lifestyle.

These exercises help you establish a higher connection with your Self at various levels. You will learn to hear or read your body and soul to understand it in an intuitive way. The messages that are trying to be conveyed constantly, but subtly, will become apparent.

This also helps you address any blockages or emotions could that come up in the future with any of the tools provided here, or those which you will learn in forthcoming volumes of the book.

Wishing you a great practice!

—Johanna Bassols

Exercise 1: Identifying the Source of Emotion

For the entire month, take notes every time you feel an emotion, especially those that repeat themselves multiple times a day: fear, anxiety, anger, happiness, love, etc. In what part of the body do you feel the emotion? Upper, middle, or lower body? Does it occur in your joints, in your chest, in your feet, etc.?

Take note of the emotion, the section of the body where it is felt, and write a brief note of what triggered the emotion, if there is any apparent cause. Also note if you ate anything immediately before the emotion arose..

Exercise 2: Tapping

Once you have identified where the emotion comes from, tap on the energy center that corresponds to that section of the body as instructed in the book or class, and take note of the physical or emotional reaction. Does the emotion or pain stop? Does it feel as strong the second time? Third time?

You can print this weekly calendar as many times as you need to complete your monthly exercise.

Day 1

Emotion				
Part of the body				
Note/food				
Tapping reaction				

Day 2

Emotion				
Part of the body				
Note/food				
Tapping reaction				

Day 3

Emotion				
Part of the body				
Note/food				
Tapping reaction				

Day 4

Emotion				
Part of the body				
Note/food				
Tapping reaction				

Day 5

Emotion				
Part of the body				
Note/food				
Tapping reaction				

Day 5

Emotion				
Part of the body				
Note/food				
Tapping reaction				

Day 6

Emotion				
Part of the body				
Note/food				
Tapping reaction				

Day 7

Emotion				
Part of the body				
Note/food				
Tapping reaction				

Exercise 3: Identifying the True Self

Make a few copies of this sheet. Complete it before and after the meditation, and see if anything has changed compared to the previous session. Repeat the meditation if needed to release more identifiers. You may notice there are some very resilient ones, or that new ones come up. Keep track of any identifiers that are deeply rooted and continue working with those until all of them have been released.

Positive identifiers	Negative identifiers

Positive identifiers	Negative identifiers

Exercise 4: Exercise to Reset and Increase the Frequency of the Electromagnetic Field

Practice three times on day one, and rest for one week, then practice again if needed. Check off the activity once completed to keep track of your progress.

Exercise 5: Exercise to Increase the Range of Expansion of the Electromagnetic Field

Practice immediately after exercise 4 and check off the activity once completed to keep track of your progress.

Week 1	1st time	2nd time	3rd time
Exercise 4			
Exercise 5			

Week 2	1st time	2nd time	3rd time
Exercise 4			
Exercise 5			

Week 3	1st time	2nd time	3rd time
Exercise 4			
Exercise 5			

Exercise 6: Releasing Stagnated Elements of the Emotional Body

Check off when completed	Date:

Exercise 7: Visualization to Reset the Emotional Body

Check off when completed	Date:

Exercise 8: Exercise to Reset the Psychosomatic Body

Complete three rounds of resetting the electric charge of the emotions in a positive memory, then do the same with the emotions coming from a thought. Check off the practice in the boxes when you've completed this activity. Repeat the same exercise a week after your initial attempt, and then a third time a week after that.

Week 1	1st / Date	2nd / Date	3rd / Date
Memory			
Thought			

Week 2	1st / Date	2nd / Date	3rd / Date
Memory			
Thought			

Week 3	1st / Date	2nd / Date	3rd / Date
Memory			
Thought			

Exercise 9: Exercise to Reset the Mental Body

Check off when completed	**Date:**

Exercise 10: Releasing the Elements of the Mental Body to Reach the "Zero" State

Check off when completed	**Date:**

Exercise 11: Awareness of the Astral Body

Practice this exercise three times per week for the next four weeks. Write the date in which you plan to practice each week to commit to that schedule. Check off the activity once you've completed it.

	Day 1:	Day 2:	Day 3:
Week 1			

	Day 1:	Day 2:	Day 3:
Week 2			

	Day 1:	Day 2:	Day 3:
Week 3			

Exercise 12: Identifying Our Energy

Check off when completed	**Date:**

Exercise 13: Exercise to Connect Our Energy Centers to the Center of the Universe

Check off when completed	**Date:**

Exercise 14: Inverting the Flow of the Energy Field to Reset it

Write down the date when you plan to practice each reset and check it off when completed. Optionally, you can write down any notes about what you experience after the reset while your elements are restructuring.

	Day 1 / Date	Day 2/ Date
Week 1		

	Day 1 / Date	Day 2/ Date
Week 2		

Exercise 15: Practicing Awareness of the All

Although you should practice this constantly, in your everyday life, this schedule is for you to commit to at least three conscious practices of "Awareness of the All" per week for the following month.

Please add the dates next to the days to set your schedule and check off the activity when completed.

	Day 1	Day 2:	Day 3:
Week 1			

	Day 1	Day 2:	Day 3:
Week 2			

	Day 1	Day 2:	Day 3:
Week 3			

	Day 1	Day 2:	Day 3:
Week 4			

Exercise 16: Exercise to Give Autonomy to the Energy Centers

Check off when completed	**Date:**

Exercise 17: Exercise to Open the Energy Centers

Check off when completed	**Date:**

Exercise 18: Exercise to Open the Energy Centers from the Physical Level

To track your progress, write down the date of your practice with each energy center, the time it took you to reach the optimal point of breathing, and how long you kept that momentum. Also record your heart rate when you were in the zone.

Week 1

Energy center	Heart	Crown	Navel
Date			
Time to opt. Point			
Duration			
Heart rate			

Note any changes in behavior or other:

Week 21

Energy center	Heart	Crown	Navel
Date			
Time to opt. Point			
Duration			
Heart rate			

Note any changes in behavior or other:

Week 3

Energy center	Heart	Crown	Navel
Date			
Time to opt. Point			
Duration			
Heart rate			

Note any changes in behavior or other:

Week 4

Energy center	Heart	Crown	Navel
Date			
Time to opt. Point			
Duration			
Heart rate			

Note any changes in behavior or other:

Exercise #19: Exercise to Recognize Your Life Purpose

You can practice this visualization at your discretion, as many times as you find necessary. However, I am adding this schedule here to set a minimum practice of once per week for the next four weeks. Please add the dates that you commit to this exercise in the boxes below and check off once completed.

	Day 1 / Date	Day 2 / Date	Day 3/ Date	Day 4 / Date
Month 1				

About the author

Johanna Bassols is the author of the Soul Reprogramming Method, a way of restructuring and reprogramming the soul by stimulating its individual elements to balance and proper functioning. She is also the founder of the Healers of the Light Academy.

She is an expert in the use of frequency words to trigger various frequencies and mental states, and an advocate for stimulating the activation of the holographic DNA and elevating the consciousness for healing purposes.

She is also an animal and environmental activist, and a firm proponent of a plant-based diet to access higher levels of consciousness.

Printed in Great Britain
by Amazon